Cooperative Learning in Action

by
Larry Holt

NATIONAL MIDDLE SCHOOL ASSOCIATION

nmsa ®
NATIONAL MIDDLE SCHOOL ASSOCIATION

Larry Holt teaches at the University of Central Florida in Orlando. A former middle level teacher, Larry continues to work with teachers in the field, and this publication is a manifestation of those efforts.

Appreciation is extended to Dr. Holt for developing this NMSA publication, to those teachers who prepared and taught these lessons, to Carolyn Fear and Martha Camomilli who typed the manuscript, and to Mary Mitchell who designed the monograph and prepared it for printing.

A special word of appreciation goes to the authors and publishers who granted permission for the reprinting of portions of their published works: David W. Johnson, Roger T. Johnson, and Edythe Holubec of Interaction Book Company, and Robert Slavin of The Johns Hopkins University.

Photographs on pages 41, 45, 83, 89, 111, and 127 are by Abe Bonowitz.

ISBN: 1-56090-066-0

Contents

PART II: LESSON STRATEGIES

Introduction

The contributions of many people have been combined with examples drawn from a number of published resources to produce this book. It is in the form of a guide for teachers interested in implementing cooperative learning.

Part I is composed of four chapters covering the basic aspects of cooperative learning. Chapter One details three classroom organizational options and the general nature of cooperative learning. Chapter Two describes the major types of cooperative groups. These techniques are presented in ample detail so that one need not have available any other resource to begin utilizing these instructional approaches. Chapter Three reviews the importance of developing the social skills needed in conjunction with cooperative groups. Chapter Four provides suggestions for getting started.

Part II of the book contains more than fifty lesson plans organized by primary subject area.

These examples of cooperative learning were submitted by teachers who use cooperative learning in their classrooms. The plans are flexible in structure and can be modified for use in any classroom. While a single grade level is often indicated, most lessons would be appropriate at other grade levels. Each has been field-tested in two middle school classrooms. Teachers can select those plans that are most appropriate for their needs and make appropriate adaptations.

The use of this resource should help middle school teachers and their students become better prepared to interact with one another in positive and effective ways. By engaging in cooperative learning, students will gain new insights about themselves, their teachers, and their peers that will enhance and promote harmony in their schools. They will gain, as well, much knowledge and ways to acquire it.

Part I
About Cooperative Learning

Research studies consistently support the academic advantages of cooperative learning.

Chapter One
Cooperative Learning: What and Why

Human beings have been successful as a species because, unlike tigers, big elephants, lizards, or gazelles who fend for themselves, we as humans are intelligent. But an intelligent man or woman in the jungle or forest would not survive alone. What has really made the human such a successful species is our ability to apply our intelligence to cooperation with others in order to accomplish group goals. Therefore, our society is composed of cooperative groups — families, neighborhoods, work groups, political parties, clubs, and teams. These groups also have a competitive element, but in all of them, if the individuals cannot cooperate to achieve a common goal, all lose out.
— Slavin, 1981, p. 655.

The school is considered a social institution that prepares children for adult roles. As a result, one would expect that cooperative activity would be emphasized in schools. Yet schools are among the institutions in our society least characterized by cooperative activity arrangements. Students traditionally work individually in schools and are constantly in competition with others for grades and for recognition. This competitive element in the school divides students into high-achieving vs. low-achieving groups that become evident soon after students enter the classroom. Those that have achieved well in the past will probably continue to achieve satisfactorily, while those that have fallen behind others will probably continue to remain behind. For many low-performing students no amount of effort will put them anywhere near the top of the class. High achievers may not work to capacity because they know they will come out with good grades regardless of whether they try hard or not. These patterns further alienate students' feelings towards school.

There have been few proposed solutions to alter the competitive nature of today's classrooms. Teachers often express their concern about this type of classroom environment, particularly as it effects low-performing students, but have felt constrained by the lack of alternatives and a general climate that supports the competitive nature of traditional schooling.

Individualization has often been touted as a replacement for competition and as a more appropriate way to learn in schools. The idea of students working individually on their own tasks, at their own pace, toward a set goal instead of competing against each other, is attractive to teachers. The overuse of the individualistic goal structure however, is hard on teachers, requires a mountain of materials, and is described by many students as the "lonely" curriculum (Johnson and Johnson, 1991). And for young adolescents it is very much contrary to their nature.

Many educators have suggested that if a combination of competition and individualization is not the answer, cooperation must be. What would happen, they ask, if teachers allowed students to work in groups to achieve a common goal? What

kind of effect might this organizational structure have on students, their achievement, and their attitudes toward school? It would probably be fun for students, would reduce the feeling of isolation, and might help solve the problem of the apparent inevitable failure for low-performing students.

Cooperation as an institutional approach to learning has its own problems. How do you keep the cooperative groups from turning out as so many have in which one student does the work for the whole group? Why should students help each other learn? Why should students care how their classmates are doing? These questions are among the common concerns expressed by teachers who are considering trying cooperative learning in their classrooms. In order to deal with the means of alleviating these and other problems associated with the use of cooperative education, it is necessary to gain a better understanding about classroom organizational structures.

Classroom Organizational Structures

An instructional skill that all teachers need to possess is knowing when and how to structure students' learning goals cooperatively, competitively, and individualistically. Each structure has its place. In the ideal classroom all three goal structures would be used at some time. All students would learn to work collaboratively with each other, compete for fun and enjoyment, and work autonomously on their own. Students would work on instructional tasks within the goal structure that is most productive for the type of task and instructional objective. Normally, teachers have the option of structuring learning tasks competitively, individualistically, or cooperatively depending on the nature of the activity and other objectives.

Competitive

In a competitive classroom situation, students work against each other to achieve a goal that only one or a few students can attain. Students are graded on a curve, which pushes them to work faster and more accurately than their peers. There is a *negative interdependence* among goal achievements because students perceive that they can obtain their goals if and only if other students in the class fail to obtain their goals (Deutsch, 1962;

Johnson & Johnson, 1987). In this situation, students try to secure an outcome that is beneficial to them but is detrimental to those with whom they are competitively linked. Unfortunately, but not surprisingly, students have come to perceive school as a predominantly competitive enterprise. Therefore, they either work hard in school to do better than other students, or they take it easy and withdraw because they do not believe they have a chance to win. Doing just enough to pass becomes the accepted mode for many such students.

Individual

In individually structured lessons students work by themselves to accomplish learning goals that are unrelated to the performance of other students. Goals are assigned each day and students' efforts are evaluated on a fixed set of standards, with rewards given accordingly. Usually, sets of material are provided for the students and they work at their own pace, ignoring the other students in the class. In individualistic learning activities, students' goal achievements are independent; students understand that the achievement of their learning goals is not related to what other students do (Deutsch, 1962; Johnson & Johnson, 1987). The accomplishment of their goals has no influence on other class members or the grades they receive. Students will seek an outcome that is personally beneficial and ignore as irrelevant the goal achievement of other students.

Cooperative

Lessons that are structured cooperatively call for students to work together to accomplish shared goals. Students in small groups are assigned material that all members of the group are to learn. Individual accountability can be checked in several ways such as randomly selecting a paper from each group to grade. In cooperative learning situations there is *positive interdependence* among students' goal attainments; students readily perceive that they can reach their learning goals if and only if other students in the learning group also reach their goals (Deutsch, 1962, Johnson & Johnson, 1987). Students seek outcomes that are beneficial to all those with whom they are cooperatively working. Students, therefore, discuss the material with each other, help one another understand it, and encourage each other to work hard.

In the 1990s, competitive and individualistic learning approaches are on the wane. The "me" classroom and "do your own thing" seatwork situation are both fading. The current trend is for "we" classrooms and "we are all in this together" learning (Johnson, Johnson, & Holubec, 1988).

Many educators who believe that they are using cooperative learning are, in fact, missing its essence. There is a crucial difference between simply putting students into groups to learn and in structuring cooperative interdependence among students. Having students side-by-side at the same table to talk with each other as they do their individual assignments is *not* cooperative learning, although such an activity has a place in the classroom. Cooperative learning is *not* assigning a report to a group of students and letting one student do all the work with the others putting their names on the product. What, then, is cooperative learning?

Cooperative learning is the instructional use of small groups so that students work together to maximize their own and each other's learning.

Five Basic Elements of Cooperative Learning

In order for teachers to successfully use cooperative learning in their classrooms, the following five basic elements advanced by Johnson, Johnson, and Holubec (1988) must be in place.

The first element is ***Positive Interdependence***. Students must perceive that they "sink or swim together." This may be achieved through mutual goals (goal interdependence); divisions of labor (task interdependence); dividing materials, resources, or information among group members (resource interdependence); assigning students roles (role interdependence); and giving joint rewards (reward interdependence). In order for a learning situation to be cooperative, students must perceive that they are positively interdependent with the other members of their learning groups.

The second element is ***Face-to-Face Interaction.*** No magic exists in positive interdependence in and of itself. Beneficial educational outcomes are due to the interaction patterns and verbal exchanges that take place among students in carefully structured cooperative learning groups. Oral summarizing, giving and receiving explanations, and elaborating (relating what is being learned to previous learning) are important types of verbal exchanges.

The third element is ***Individual Accountability.*** Cooperative learning groups are not successful until every member has learned the material or has helped with and understands the assignment. Thus, it is important to frequently stress and assess individual learning so that group members can appropriately support and help each other. Some ways of structuring individual accountability are by giving each group member an individual exam or randomly selecting one member to give an answer for the entire group.

The fourth element is ***Interpersonal and Small Group Skills.*** Rarely do students come to school with the social skills they need to collaborate effectively with others; so teachers need to teach the appropriate communication, leadership, trust, decision-making, and conflict management skills to students and provide the motivation to use these skills in order for groups to function effectively.

The last basic element is ***Group Processing.*** Processing means giving students the time and procedures to analyze how well their groups are functioning and how well they are using the necessary social skills. This processing helps all group members achieve while maintaining effective working relationships among members. Feedback from the teacher and/or student observers on how well they observed the groups working may help in processing effectiveness. (p. 23)

Teachers are interested in having students acquire the abilities to maximize their learning, hold positive attitudes toward school, and think critically. Although these are all important expectations of the students we teach, cooperation is as basic to human survival as the air we breathe. The ability of individuals to work collaboratively with others is the keystone to building and maintaining stable marriages, families, careers, friendships, and communities (Johnson, Johnson, & Holubec, 1988). Possessing the skills of reading, speaking, listening, writing,

computing, and problem-solving are of little value if the person cannot apply them in cooperative interaction with other people. People today, whether engineers, secretaries, accountants, teachers, mechanics, or medical professionals, will be required to work cooperatively on the job as well as in their families and communities.

As humans, we are an intelligent species because we know the value and importance of effective communication, collaborative working relationships, and teamwork. Schools, however, have not done an adequate job of preparing our youth for the realities of life because they have seldom provided students with opportunities to work cooperatively in groups. The most logical way to correct this situation and to ensure that students gain the cooperative skills required in most task-oriented situations is by structuring academic learning situations cooperatively.

Cooperative learning is not a new idea. Throughout history, those individuals who could organize and coordinate their efforts to achieve a common purpose have been most successful in virtually every human endeavor. However, simply placing students in groups and telling them to work together does not in and of itself achieve the competence in cooperation that is needed. Chapter

Two will distinguish between traditional and cooperative learning situations and detail the major types of cooperative learning.

References

Deutsch, M. (1962). Cooperation and trust: Some theoretical notes. In M.R. Jones (Ed.), *Nebraska symposium on motivation.* (pp. 275-319). Lincoln, NE: University of Nebraska Press.

Johnson, D.W., & Johnson, F. (1987). *Joining together: Group theory and group skills* (3rd ed.). Englewood Cliffs, NJ: Prentice-Hall, Inc.

Johnson & Johnson, (1991). Chapter 14. In Waxman/Walberg (1990). *Effective teaching: Current research.* Berkeley, CA: McCutchan Publishing Company.

Johnson, D.W., Johnson, R.T. & Holubec, E. (1988). *Cooperation in the classroom.* Edina, MN: Interaction Book Company.

Slavin, R., (1981). Synthesis of research on cooperative learning. *Educational Leadership.* May, pp. 655-658.

The exuberance of early adolescents is often released as groups share the results of their academic activities.

Chapter Two
Types of Cooperative Learning

Types of Cooperative Learning

Cooperative learning is not limited to use in any grade level or content area. In fact, most cooperative learning structures can be successfully used beginning in grade two and continuing through higher education. Within a classroom, a teacher can use both *informal* and *formal groups*. A formal group exists when the group is given an assignment to complete and stays together for an extended period, even for several weeks. An informal group exists when a group is given an assignment for a short discussion task and may stay together for only a few minutes. Another grouping structure is the *base group*. Base groups are long-term groups who stay together for at least one semester and whose purpose is primarily to provide peer support and accountability as needed.

Informal cooperative learning groups are temporary ad hoc groups that last from a few minutes to one class period. These groups are designed to:

- focus the students' attention on the material to be learned,

- set a mood conducive to learning,

- help organize in advance the material to be covered in a class session,

- ensure that students cognitively process the material being taught,

- provide closure to an instructional session.

Informal cooperative learning groups are often organized so that students can engage in focused discussions before and after a formal presentation of material and also by interspercing "turn to your partner" discussions throughout a lecture. The information presented by the instructor is then more likely to be understood by the students, and some of the problems of the traditional lecture are overcome.

Formal cooperative learning groups may last from one class period to several weeks of instruction focused on one specific task or assignment (i.e., solving a set of problems, completing a major unit, writing a report, or conducting an investigation). The teacher has the option of formulating a class assignment to be cooperative. To establish formal cooperative learning groups, the teacher:

- decides on group size and how to assign students to groups,

- presents the academic concepts, principles and strategies to the whole class,

- assigns a task to be completed cooperatively in groups,

- monitors the functioning of the learning groups and intervenes,

- teaches collaborative skills,

- provides assistance when needed.

Students are taught to look to their peers for assistance, feedback, reinforcement, and support. Students are expected to share materials, interact, and encourage each other's academic performance. They can orally explain to one another what was taught and elaborate on the strategies and concepts. In this way, students hold each other accountable for completing the assignment.

Base groups are long-term, *heterogeneous* cooperative learning groups (e.g., a group might

consist of one high, one low, and two average academic level students). Base groups are designed to support, help, assist, and encourage members to make academic progress, while members develop cognitively and socially in healthy ways. The schedule needs to be arranged so that the group stays together for much of the day and regularly works together to complete cooperative learning   tasks. This makes it possible to meet and discuss the academic progress of each member, provide help and assistance to each other, and verify that each member is completing the academic assignments.

Base groups may also be given the responsibility of letting group members who have been absent know what went on in the class during their absence. The use of base groups tends to improve attendance, personalize both the required work and the school experience, and improve the quality and quantity of learning (Johnson and Johnson, 1991).

Cooperative learning promotes higher level thinking that is most clearly seen in conceptual learning and problem-solving tasks. Cooperation, cognition, and metacognition are all intimately related. Cooperative learning provides the context within which cognition and metacognition best take place. The oral and interpersonal exchanges between group members and the intellectual challenges that result from conflicting ideas and conclusions promote critical thinking, higher-level reasoning, and metacognitive thought. The divergent thinking and inspiration that sparks creativity results from the oral explanations and elaboration required within cooperative learning groups. Explaining what one knows to one's group-mates facilitates the understanding of how to apply knowledge and skills to work and community settings (Johnson and Johnson, 1991).

Roles Within the Group

To ensure that students are individually accountable, roles must be assigned. The various roles that are needed to ensure an effective group can be assigned by the teacher as needs arise. As students begin working in groups, members learn how these roles can complement and interconnect with the task at hand. Usually the roles are rotated so that each student obtains experience in each role. Roles are assigned to create positive interdependence and to teach students new skills. Both working and social skills roles are included. Students will learn new roles if those roles are carefully defined, watched for, and rewarded.

The following role definitions taken from Johnson, Johnson, and Houlbec (1988) are ones commonly used.

Reader: Reads the material out loud to the group, carefully and with expression, so that group members can understand and remember it.

Writer/Recorder: Carefully records the best answers of the group on the worksheet or paper, edits what the group has written, gets the group members to check and sign the paper, then turns it in to the teacher.

Materials Handler: Gets any materials or equipment needed by the group, keeps track of them, and puts them away carefully.

Encourager: Watches to make certain that everyone is participating and invites reluctant or silent members to contribute. Sample statements: "Jane, what do you think?" "Robert, do you have anything to add?" "Pedro, help us out." "Leroy, what are your ideas on this?"

Checker: Checks on the comprehension or learning of group members by asking them to explain or summarize material discussed. Sample statements: "Terry, why did we decide on this answer for number two?" "James, explain how we got this answer." "Anne, summarize for us what we've decided here."

Praiser: Helps members feel good about their contributions to the group by telling them how helpful they are. This role is good to help combat "put downs." Sample statements: "That's a good idea, Al." "Sharon, You're very helpful." "Karen, I like the way you've helped us." "Good job, John."

Prober: In a pleasant way, keeps the group from superficially answering by not allowing the members to agree too quickly. Agrees when satisfied that the group has explored all the possibilities. Sample statements: "What other possibilities are there for this problem or question?" "What else could we put here?" "Let's double check that answer."

Relater/Elaboration Seeker: This person's job is to relate new information presented in today's lesson with what has already been presented. Sample statements: "How does this compare with what we already know?" "What is the purpose behind what we have just learned?" "How does this relate?" (p. 17)

There are other roles that can be assigned, depending on the needs of the group. Additionally, roles that are non-working roles can be assigned to increase social skills awareness among group members. Some social skills roles might include: *Noise Monitor* (uses nonverbal signal to quiet the group down), *Energizer* (energizes the group when it starts lagging), *Observer* (to keep track of how well the team members are collaborating), *Asker*

for Help, Timekeeper, Question Asker, and *Paraphraser.*

The following descriptions of the three major plans, Student Teams-Achievement Divisions (STAD), Teams-Games-Tournaments (TGT), and Jigsaw, are included largely in the words of their creators.

STUDENT TEAMS - ACHIEVEMENT DIVISIONS (STAD)

STAD and TGT are similar methods, both primarily applicable to grades 2-12. The only difference between them is that STAD uses quizzes to assess student learning while TGT uses games. The major components of these methods are depicted in Figure 1.

Student Team Learning Methods

Figure 1. Basic Schedule of Activities for STAD and TGT

OVERVIEW

STAD is made up of five major components: class presentations, teams, quizzes, individual improvement scores, and team recognition. These components are described below.

Class Presentations. Material in STAD is initially introduced in a class presentation. This is most often direct instruction or a lecture-discussion conducted by the teacher, but could include audio-visual presentations. Class presentations in STAD differ from usual teaching only in that they must be clearly focused on the STAD unit. In this way, students realize that they must pay careful attention during the class presentation, because doing so will help them to do well on the quizzes, and their quiz scores determine their team scores.

Teams. Teams are composed of four or five students who represent a cross-section of the class in academic performance, sex, and race or ethnicity. The major function of the team is to prepare its members to do well on the quizzes. After the teacher presents the material, the team meets to study worksheets or other material. The worksheets are usually teacher-made. Most often, the study takes the form of students discussing problems together, comparing answers, and correcting any misconceptions if teammates make mistakes.

The team is the most important feature of STAD. At every point, emphasis is placed on team members doing their best for the team, and on the team doing its best to help its members. The team provides the peer support for academic performance that is important for effects on learning, and the team provides the mutual concern and respect that are important for effects on such outcomes as intergroup relations, self-esteem, and acceptance of mainstreamed students.

Quizzes. After one to two periods of teacher presentation and one to two periods of team practice, the students take individual quizzes. Students are not permitted to help one another during the quizzes. This ensures that every student is individually responsible for knowing the material.

Individual Improvement Scores. The idea

behind the individual improvement scores is to give each student a performance goal that the student can reach, but only if he or she works harder and performs better than in the past. Any student can contribute maximum points to his or her team in this scoring system, but no student can do so without showing improvement over past performance. Each student is given a "base" score, derived from the student's average performance on similar quizzes. Then students earn points for their teams based on how much their quiz scores exceed their base scores.

Team Recognition. Teams may earn certificates or other rewards if their average scores exceed a certain criterion. Students' team scores may also be used to determine up to 20% of their grades.

PREPARING TO USE STAD

Materials. STAD can be used with curriculum materials specifically designed by individual teachers.

It is quite easy to make your own materials. Simply make a worksheet, a worksheet answer sheet, and a quiz for each unit you plan to teach. Each unit should occupy three to five days of instruction.

Assigning Students to Teams. A team in STAD is a group of four or five students who represent a cross section of the class in past performance, race or ethnicity, and sex. That is, a four-person team in a class that is one-half male, one-half female, and three-quarters white, one-quarter minority might have two boys and two girls and three white students and one minority student. The team would also have a high performer, a low performer, and two average performers. Of course, "high performer" is a relative term; it means high for the class, not necessarily high compared to national norms.

Students are assigned to teams by the teacher, rather than by choosing teams themselves, because students tend to choose others like themselves. You may take likes, dislikes, and "deadly combinations" of students into account in your assignments, but do not let students choose their own teams. Instead follow these steps:

1. ***Make Copies of Team Summary Sheets.***

Before you begin to assign students to teams, you will need to make one copy of a Team Summary Sheet (Figure 5) for every four students in your class.

2. *Rank Students.* On a sheet of paper, rank the students in your class from highest to lowest in past performance. Use whatever information you have to do this — test scores are best, grades are good, but your own judgment is fine. It may be difficult to be exact in your ranking, but do the best you can.

3. *Decide on the Number of Teams.* Each team should have four members if possible. To decide how many teams you will have, divide the number of students in the class by four. If the number is divisible by four, the quotient will be the number of four-member teams you should have. For example, if there are 32 students in the class, you would have eight teams with four members each.

If the division is uneven, the remainder will be one, two, or three, You will then have one, two, or three teams composed of five members. For example, if there are thirty students in your class, you would have seven teams; five teams would have four members and two would have five members.

4. *Assign Students to Teams.* When you are assigning students to teams, balance the teams so that (a) each team is composed of students whose performance levels range from low to average to high, and (b) the average performance level of all the teams in the class is about equal. To assign students to teams, use your list of students ranked by performance. Assign team letters to each student. For example, in an eight-team class you would use the letters A through H. Start at the top of your list with the letter "A;" continue lettering toward the middle. When you get to the last team letter, continue lettering in the opposite order. For example if you were using the letters A-H (as in Figure 2), the eighth and ninth students would be assigned to Team H, the tenth to Team G, the next to Team F, and so on. When you get back to letter "A," stop and repeat the process from the bottom up, again starting and ending with the letter "A."

Notice that two of the students (17 and 18) in

Figure 2 are not assigned at this point. They will be added to teams as fifth members, but first the teams should be checked for race or ethnicity and sex balance. If, for example, one-fourth of the class is black, approximately one student on each team should be black. If the teams you have made based on performance ranking are not evenly divided on both ethnicity and sex (they will hardly ever be balanced on the first try), you should change team assignments by trading students of the same approximate performance level, but of different ethnicity or sex, between teams until a balance is achieved.

5. *Fill Out Team Summary Sheets.* After you have finished assigning all students to teams, fill in the names of the students on each team on your Team Summary Sheets, leaving the "team name" blank.

Figure 2. Assigning Students to Teams

	Rank Order	Team Name
High-performing Students	1	A
	2	B
	3	C
	4	D
	5	E
	6	F
	7	G
	8	H
Average-performing Students	9	H
	10	G
	11	F
	12	E
	13	D
	14	C
	15	B
	16	A
	17	
	18	
	19	A
	20	B
	21	C
	22	D
	23	E
	24	F
	25	G
	26	H
Students	27	H
	28	G
	29	F
	30	E
	31	D
	32	C
	33	B
	34	A

Determining Initial Base Scores. Base scores represent students' average scores on past quizzes. If you are starting STAD after you have given three or more quizzes, use students' average quiz scores as base scores. Otherwise, use students' final grades from the previous year (see Figure 3).

Figure 3. Determining Initial Base Scores	
Last Year's Grade	Initial Base Score
A	90
A-/B+	85
B	80
B-/C+	75
C	70
C-/D+	65
D	60
F	55

AVERAGE THREE TEST SCORES

Sara's Scores	90
	84
	87
	$261 \div 3 = 87$
Sara's Base Score	87

SCHEDULE OF ACTIVITIES

STAD consists of a regular cycle of instructional activities, as follows:

Teach — present the lesson

Team Study — Students work on worksheets in their teams to master the material

Test — Students take individual quizzes

Team Recognition — Team scores are computed based on team members' improvements scores, and individual certificates, a class newsletter, or a bulletin board recognize high-scoring teams.

These activities are described in detail below.

Teach

Time:	1-2 class periods
Main Idea:	Present the lesson
Materials Needed:	Your lesson plan

Each lesson in STAD begins with a class presentation. The class presentation should cover the opening development and guided practice components of your total lesson, while the team activities and quiz cover independent practice and assessment respectively. In your lesson, stress the following:

Opening

- Tell students what they are about to learn and why it is important. Arouse student curiosity with a puzzling demonstration, real-life problem, or other means.

- Briefly review any prerequisite skills or information.

Development

- Stick close to the objectives that you will test.

- Focus on meaning, not memorization.

- Actively demonstrate concepts or skills, using visual aids, manipulatives, and many examples.

- Frequently assess student comprehension by asking many questions.

- Always explain why an answer is correct or incorrect unless it is obvious.

- Move rapidly from concept to concept as soon as students have grasped the main idea.

- Maintain momentum by eliminating interruptions, asking many questions, and moving rapidly through the lesson.

Guided Practice

- Have all students work problems or examples or prepare answers to your questions.

- Call on students at random so that they will never know to whom you might direct a question—this makes all students prepare themselves to answer.

- Do not give long class assignments at this point — have students work one or two problems or examples or prepare one or two answers, then give them feedback.

Team Study

<u>Time:</u> 1-2 class periods

<u>Main Idea:</u> Students study worksheets in their teams

<u>Materials Needed:</u>

- two worksheets for every team

- two answer sheets for every team

During team study, the team members' tasks are to master the material you presented in your lesson and to help their teammates master the material. Students have worksheets and answer sheets they can use to practice the skill being taught and to assess themselves and their teammates. Only two copies of the worksheets and answer sheets are given to each team, to force teammates to work together, but if some students prefer to work alone or want their own copies, you may make additional copies available.

Many teachers like to engage students in team-building activities before beginning team work, while others just start in. If you wish to give your students some experience working as a team before they start working in teams, see Chapter Three.

On the first day of team work in STAD, you should explain to students what it means to work in teams. In particular, discuss the following team rules (which you may list on a bulletin board or chalkboard):

Team Rules

1. Students have a responsibility to make sure that their teammates have learned the material.

2. No one is finished studying until all teammates have mastered the subject.

3. Ask all teammates for help before asking the teacher.

4. Teammates may talk to each other softly.

Present and discuss the team rules before beginning team work. Students may be encouraged to add additional rules if they like. Then proceed with the introduction of team work.

- Have teammates move their desks together or move to team tables.

- Give teams a few minutes to choose a team name. Any teams that cannot agree on a name in the time given may choose one later.

- Hand out worksheets and answer sheets (two of each per team) with a minimum of fuss.

- Tell students to work together in pairs or threes. If they are working problems, (as in math), each student in a pair or triad should work the problem individually, and then check with his or her partner(s). If anyone missed a question, teammates have a responsibility to explain it. If students are working on short-answer questions, they may quiz each other, with partners taking turns holding the answer sheet or attempting to answer the questions.

- Emphasize to students that they are not finished studying until they are sure their teammates will make 100% on the quiz. Make sure students understand that the worksheets are for studying — not merely for filling out and handing in. That is why it is important for students to have answer sheets to check themselves and teammates as they study.

- Have students explain answers to one another instead of just checking each other against the answer sheet.

- Remind students that if they have questions, they must ask all teammates before asking you.

- While students are working in teams, circulate through the class, praising teams that are working well, sitting in with each team to hear how they are doing, and so on.

Test

Time: 1/2-1 class period

Main Idea: Individual quiz

Material Needed: One quiz per student

- Distribute the quiz and give students adequate time to complete it. Do not let students work together on the quiz; at this point students must show what they have learned as individuals. Have students move their desks apart if possible.

- Either allow students to exchange papers with members of other teams, or collect the quizzes to score after class. Be sure to have quizzes scored and team scores figured in time for the next class if at all possible.

Team Recognition

Main Idea: Figure individual improvement scores and team scores, and present certificates or other team awards.

FIGURING INDIVIDUAL AND TEAM SCORES

As soon as possible after each quiz, you should figure individual improvement scores and team scores and reward high-scoring teams. If at all possible, the announcement of team scores should be made in the first period after the quiz. This makes the connection between doing well and receiving recognition clear to students and increases their motivation to do their best.

Improvement Points. Students earn points for their teams based on the degree to which their quiz scores (percent correct) exceed their base scores:

Quiz Score	Improvement Points
More than 10 points below base score	0
10 points below to 1 point below base score	10
Base score to 10 points above base score	20
More than 10 points above base scores	30
Perfect paper (regardless of base score)	30

Before you begin to figure improvement points, you will need one copy of a Quiz Score Sheet. Figuring improvement points is not at all difficult, and when you get used to it, it will take only a few minutes. Figure 4 shows how improvement points would be computed for one set of students. The purpose of base scores and improvement points is to make it possible for all students to bring maximum points to their teams, whatever their level of past performance. Students understand that it is fair that each student should be compared to his or her own level of past performance, as all students enter class with different levels of skills and experience in mathematics.

Put the points you have calculated on each student's quiz as follows: Base Score = 83; Quiz Score = 90; Improvement Points = 20. Put the improvement points on students' Team Summary Sheets (see Figure 5).

Team Scores. To figure team scores, put each student's improvement points on the appropriate Team Summary Sheet and divide by the number of team members who were present, rounding off any fractions. See Figure 5. Note that team scores depend on improvement scores rather than on raw quiz scores.

RECOGNIZING TEAM ACCOMPLISHMENTS

Criteria for awards. There are three levels of awards given based on average team scores.

Criterion Team Average	Award
15	*Goodteam*
20	*Greatteam*
25	*Superteam*

Note that all teams can achieve the awards; teams are not in competition with one another.

The above criteria are set so that to be a *Greatteam,* most team members scored above their base scores, and to be a *Superteam,* most team members scored at least ten points above their base scores. You may change these criteria if necessary.

You should provide some sort of recognition or reward for achieving at the *Greatteam* or *Superteam* level. Attractive certificates to each team member may be used, with a large, fancy certificate (8 1/2" x 11") for *Superteams* and a smaller one for *Greatteams*. *Goodteams* should just receive congratulations in class. Many teachers make bulletin board displays listing the week's *Superteams* and *Greatteams*, or displaying Polaroid pictures of the successful teams. Others prepare one-page newsletters, give students special buttons to wear, or let *Superteams* and *Greatteams* line up first for recess or receive other special privileges. Use your imagination and creativity, and vary rewards from time to time; it is more important that *you* are excited about students' accomplishments than that you give large rewards.

RETURNING THE FIRST SET OF QUIZZES

When you return the first set of quizzes (with the base scores, quiz scores, and improvement points) to the students, you will need to explain the improvement point system. In your explanation, emphasize three points:

1. The main purpose of the improvement point system is to give everyone a minimum score to try to beat and to set that minimum score based on past performance so that all students will have an equal chance to be successful if they do their best academically.

2. The second purpose of the improvement point system is to make students realize that the scores of everyone on their team are important — that all members of the team can earn maximum improvement points if they do their best.

3. The improvement point system is fair because everyone is competing only with himself or herself — trying to improve his or her own performance — regardless of what the rest of the class does.

RECOMPUTING BASE SCORES

Every marking period (or more frequently, if you like), recompute students' average quiz scores on all quizzes and assign students new base scores.

CHANGING TEAMS

After five or six weeks of STAD, reassign students to new teams. This gives students who were on low-scoring teams a new chance, allows students to work with other classmates, and keeps the program fresh.

GRADING

When it comes time to give students report card grades, the grades should be based on the students' actual quiz scores, not their improvement points or team scores. If you wish, you might make the students' team scores a part of their grades (up to 20% of their grades might be determined by team scores). If your school gives separate grades for effort, you might use team and/or improvement scores to determine the effort grades.

Figure 4. Quiz Score Sheet (STAD and Jigsaw II)

| Student | Date May 23 | | | Date | | | Date | | |
| | Quiz Addition with Regrouping | | | Quiz | | | Quiz | | |
	Base Score	Quiz Score	Improvement Points	Base Score	Quiz Score	Improvement Points	Base Score	Quiz Score	Improvement Points
Sara A.	90	100	30						
Tom B.	90	100	30						
Ursula C.	90	82	10						
Danielle D.	85	74	0						
Eddie E.	85	98	30						
Natasha F.	85	82	10						

Figure 5. Team Summary Sheet

Team Members	1	2	3	4	5	6	7	8	9	10	11	12	13	14
Sara A.														
Eddie E.														
Edgar I.														
Carol N.														
Total Team Score														
Team Average														
Team Award	Super Team													

Team Name Fantastic Four

TEAMS — GAMES — TOURNAMENTS (TGT)

OVERVIEW

TGT is the same as STAD in every respect but one: instead of the quizzes and the individual improvement score system, TGT uses academic game tournaments, in which students compete as representatives of their teams with members of other teams who are like them in past academic performance. A description of the components of TGT follows.

Class Presentations. (Same as for STAD)

Teams. (Same as for STAD)

Games. The games are composed of content-relevant questions designed to test the knowledge students gain from class presentations and team practice. Games are played at tables of three students, each of whom represents a different team. Most games are simply numbered questions on a ditto sheet. A student picks a number card and attempts to answer the question corresponding to the number. A challenge rule permits players to challenge each other's answers.

Tournaments. The tournament is the structure in which the games take place. It is usually held at the end of the week, after the teacher has made a class presentation and the teams have had time to practice with the worksheets. For the first tournament, the teacher assigns students to tournament tables — assigning the top three students in past performance to Table 1, the next three to Table 2, and so on. This equal competition, like the individual improvement score system in STAD, makes it possible for students of all levels of past performance to contribute maximally to their team scores if they do their best. Figure 6 illustrates the relationship between heterogeneous teams and homogeneous tournament tables.

After the first week, students change tables depending on their own performance in the most recent tournament. The winner at each table is "bumped up" to the next higher table (e.g., from Table 6 to Table 5); the second scorer stays at the same table; and the low scorer is "bumped down." In this way, if students have been mis-assigned at first, they will eventually be moved up or down until they reach their true level of performance.

Team Recognition. (Same as for STAD)

PREPARING TO USE TGT

Materials. Curriculum materials for TGT are the same as for STAD. Also needed will be one set of cards numbered from 1 to 30 for every three students in your largest class. Teachers can make their own by numbering colored index cards.

Figure 6. Assignment to Tournament Tables

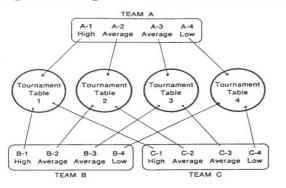

Assigning Students to Teams. Assign students to four- to five-member heterogeneous teams exactly as for STAD.

Assigning Students to Initial Tournament Tables. Make a copy of the Tournament Table Assignment Sheet. On it, list students from top to bottom in past performance in the same ranking used to form teams (see Figure 2). Count the number of students in the class. If the number is divisible by three, all tournament tables will have three members; just assign the first three students on the list to Table 1, the next three to Table 2, and so on. If there is a remainder to the division, one or two of the top tournament tables will have four members. For example, a class of 29 students will have nine tournament tables, two of which will have four members. The first four students on the ranked list will be assigned to Table 1, the next four to Table 2, and three to other tables (see Figure 7).

Figure 7. Tournament Table Assignment Sheet (TGT)

Tournament number:

Student	Team	1	2	3	4	5	6	7	8	9	10	11	12	13
Sam	Orioles	1												
Sarah	Cougars	1												
Tyrone	Whiz Kids	1												
Maria	Geniuses	2												
Liz	Orioles	2												
John T.	Cougars	2												
Sylvia	Whiz Kids	3												
Tom	Geniuses	3												
John F.	Orioles	3												
Tanya	Whiz Kids	4												
Carla	Orioles	4												
Kim	Cougars	4												
Carlos	Geniuses	4												
Shirley	Whiz Kids	5												
Ralph	Cougars	5												
Ruth	Geniuses	5												

HOW TO START TGT

Begin with the schedule of activities described in the following section. After teaching the lesson, announce team assignments and have students move their desks together to make team tables. Tell students that they will be working in teams for several weeks and competing in academic games to add points to their team scores, and the highest scoring teams will receive recognition in a class newsletter.

SCHEDULE OF ACTIVITIES

TGT consists of a regular cycle of instructional activities, as follows:

TEACH — present the lesson.

TEAM STUDY — Students work on worksheets in their teams to master the material.

TOURNAMENTS — Students play academic games in ability-homogeneous, three-member tournament tables.

TEAM RECOGNITION — Team scores are computed based on team members' tournament scores, and a class newsletter or bulletin board recognizes high-scoring teams.

These activities are described in detail on the following pages.

Teach

Time: 1-2 class periods

Main Idea: Present the lesson

Materials Needed: Your lesson plan

See the section on Teaching for STAD, page 12.

Team Study

Time: 1-2 class periods

Main Idea: Students study worksheets in their teams.

Materials Needed: Two worksheets for every team and two answer sheets for every team.

See the section on Team Study for STAD, page 18.

Tournaments

Time: One class period

Main Idea: Students compete at three-member, ability-homogeneous tournament tables.

Materials Needed:

Tournament Table Assignment Sheet, with tournament table assignments filled in.

One copy of Game Sheet and Game Answers (same as the quiz and quiz answers for STAD) for each tournament table.

One Game Score Sheet for each tournament table.

One deck of number cards to correspond to the number of questions on the Game Sheet for each tournament table.

At the beginning of the tournament period, announce students' tournament table assignments and have them move desks together or go to tables serving as tournament tables. Have selected students help distribute one game sheet, one answer sheet, one deck of number cards, and one game score sheet to each table. Then begin the game.

To start the game, the students draw cards to determine the first reader — the student drawing the highest number. Play proceeds in a clockwise direction from the first reader.

TGT Game Rules

Reader
1. Picks a numbered card and finds the corresponding question on the game sheet.
2. Reads the question out loud.
3. Tries to answer

1st challenger

Challenges if he or she wants to (and gives a different answer), or passes.

2nd challenger

Challenges if 1st challenger passes, if he or she wants to. When all have challenged or passed, 2nd challenger checks the answer sheet. Whoever was *right* keeps the card. If the *reader* was wrong, he or she must put a previously won card, if any, back in the deck.

When the game begins, the reader shuffles the cards and picks the top one. He or she then reads aloud the question corresponding to the number on the card, including the possible answers if the question is multiple choice. For example, a student who picks card number 21 answers question number 21. A reader who is not sure of the answer is allowed to guess without penalty. If the content of the game involves math problems, all students (not just the reader) should work the problems so that they will be ready to challenge. After the reader gives an answer, the student to his or her left (first challenger) has the option of challenging, and giving a different answer. If he or she passes, or if the second challenger has an answer different from the first two, the second challenger may challenge. Challengers have to be careful, however, because they lose a card (if they have one) if

they are wrong. When everyone has answered, challenged, or passed, the second challenger (or the player to the reader's right) checks the answer sheet and reads the right answer aloud. They player who gave the right answer keeps the card. If either challenger gave a wrong answer, he or she must return a previously won card (if any) to the deck. If no one gave a right answer, the card returns to the deck.

For the next round, everything moves one position to the left - the first challenger becomes the reader, the second challenger becomes the first challenger, and the reader becomes the second challenger. Play continues, as determined by the teacher, until the period ends or the deck is exhausted. When the game is over, players record the number of cards they won on the Game Score Sheet in the column marked "Game 1." If there is time, students reshuffle the deck and play a second game, recording the number of cards won under "Game 2," on the score sheet. (See Figure 8.)

Figure 8. Sample Game

TABLE # _____   GAME SCORE SHEET   ROUND # _____

Player	Team	Game 1	Game 2	Game 3	Day's Total	Tournament Points
Eric	Giants	5	7		12	20
Lisa A.	Geniuses	14	10		24	60
Darryl	B. Bombs	11	12		23	40

All students should play the game at the same time. While they are playing, the teacher should move from group to group to answer questions and make sure that everyone understands the game procedures. Ten minutes before the end of the period, call "time" and have students stop and count their cards. They should then fill in their names, teams, and scores on the Game Score Sheet, as in Figure 8.

Have students add up the scores they earned in each game (if they played more than one) and fill in their day's total. For younger children (fourth grade or below), simply collect the score sheets. If students are older, have them calculate their tournament points. Figure 9 summarizes tournament points for all possible outcomes. In general, have students give the top scorer sixty points, the second scorer forty points, and the third scorer twenty points at a three-person table with no ties. If there are more or less than three players or if there are any ties, use Figure 9 to tell students what to do. When everyone has calculated his or her tournament points, have a student collect the Game Score Sheets.

Team Recognition

Main Idea: Figure team scores and prepare a class newsletter or bulletin board as a means of recognizing team achievement.

FIGURING TEAM SCORES

As soon as possible after the tournament, figure team scores and prepare team certificates or write a class newsletter to announce the standings. To do this, first check the tournament points on the Game Score Sheets. Then, simply transfer each student's tournament points to the Team Summary Sheet for his or her team, add all the team members' scores and divide by the number of team members present. Figure 10 shows the recording and totaling of scores for one team.

RECOGNIZING TEAM ACCOMPLISHMENTS

As in STAD, there are three levels of awards given based on average team scores.

Criterion Team Average	Award
15	*Goodteam*
20	*Greatteam*
25	*Superteam*

You may give certificates to teams that meet greatteam or superteam criteria. *Goodteams* should just be congratulated in class. Instead of or in addition to team certificates, you may wish to make bulletin board displays, recognizing each week's successful teams, posting their pictures or team names in a place of honor. Many teachers use class newsletters in TGT. Whatever means you use of recognizing team accomplishments, it is important that you communicate that team success (not just individual success) is what is important, as this provides the motivation to students to help their teammates learn.

BUMPING: REASSIGNING STUDENTS TO TOURNAMENT TABLES

Bumping, or reassigning students to new tournament tables, must be done after each tournament to prepare for the next tournament. It is easiest to do the bumping when figuring team scores.

To "bump" students, use the steps which follow. Figure 11 shows a diagram of the bumping procedure, and the next figure gives an example of a completed Tournament Table Assignment Sheet, showing how the bumping procedure works for a hypothetical class after two tournaments (one tournament per week).

1. Use the Game Score Sheets to identify the high and low scorers at their tables. If there was a tie for high score at any table, flip a coin to decide which number to circle; do not circle more than one number per table. In Figure 12, Tyrone, Maria, Tom, Carla, and Ralph were table winners in the first tournament, so their table numbers are circled in the first column; Tyrone and other winners in the second tournament have their numbers are circled in the second column.

Figure 9. Calculating Tournament Points

FOR A FOUR-PLAYER GAME

Player	No Ties	Tie for Top	Tie for Middle	Tie for Low	3-Way Tie for Top	3-Way Tie for Low	4-Way Tie	Tie for Low and High
Top Scorer	60 points	50	60	60	50	60	40	50
High Middle Scorer	40 points	50	40	40	50	30	40	50
Low Middle Scorer	30 points	30	40	30	50	30	40	30
Low Scorer	20 points	20	20	30	20	30	40	30

FOR A THREE-PLAYER GAME

Player	No Ties	Tie for Top Score	Tie for Low Score	3-Way Tie
Top Scorer	60 points	50	60	40
Middle Scorer	40 points	50	30	40
Low Scorer	20 points	20	30	40

FOR A TWO-PLAYER GAME

Player	No Ties	Tied
Top Scorer	60	40
Low Scorer	20	40

Figure 10. Sample Team Summary Sheet

TEAM NAME: Geniuses
TEAM SUMMARY SHEET

Team Members	1	2	3	4	5	6	7	8	9	10	11	12	13	14
Mark	60	20	20	40										
Kevin	40	40	20	60										
Lisa A.	50	20	40	60										
John F.	60	60	20	40										
Dewanda	40	40	60	20										
Total Team Score	250	180	160	220										
*Team Average	50	36	32	44										
Team Award		Superteam		Goodteam										

*Team Average = Total Team Score / Number of Team Members

21

2. Underline the table numbers of students who were low scorers. Again, if there was a tie for low score at any table, flip a coin to decide which to underline; do not underline more than one number per table. In Figure 12, Sarah, John T., John F., Kim, and Shirley were low scorers at their respective tables in the first tournament.

3. Leave all other table assignments as they were, including numbers for absent student.

4. In the column for the next tournament, transfer the numbers as follows:

If the number is *circled*, reduce it by one (4 becomes 3), This means that the winner at Table 4 will compete at Table 3 the next week, a table where the competition will be more difficult. The only exception is that 1 remains 1, because Table is the highest table. If the number is *underlined*, increase it by one (4 becomes 5), except at the lowest table, where the low scorer stays at the same table (e.g., 10 remains 10). This means that the low scorer at each table will compete the next week at a table where the competition will be less difficult. If the number is neither underlined nor circled, do not change it for the next tournament — transfer the same number.

In Figure 12, note that Tom won at Table 3 in the first tournament and was bumped up to Table 2. At Table 2 he was the low scorer, so for the third week's tournament he will compete at Table 3 again. Sylvia was the middle scorer at Table 3 in the first tournament, so she stayed at Table 3; then she lost in the second tournament and was moved to Table 4.

Count the number of students assigned to each table for the next week's tournament. Most tables should have three students; as many as two may have four. If table assignments do not work out this way, make some changes so that they do.

Note that Figure 12, Tyrone won twice at Table 1, but did not change tables because there was no higher place to go than Table 1. Shirley and Kim lost at Table 5, but were not "bumped down" because Table 5 was the lowest table.

Changing Teams

After five or six weeks of TGT, assign students to new teams.

Combining TGT with Other Activities

Teachers may wish to use TGT for part of their instruction, and other methods for other parts. For example, a science teacher might use TGT three days a week to teach basic science concepts, but then use related laboratory exercises on the other two days. TGT can also be used in combination with STAD, either by alternating quizzes one week and tournaments the next, or by having a quiz on the day after each tournament and counting both the quiz score and the tournament score toward the team score. This procedure gives the teacher a better idea of student progress than the tournament alone.

Grading

TGT does not automatically produce scores that can be used to compute individual grades. If this is a serious problem, consider using STAD instead of TGT. To determine individual grades, many teachers using TGT give a midterm and a final test each semester; some give a quiz after each tournament. Students' grades should be based on quiz scores or other individual assessments, not on tournament points or team scores. However, students' tournament points and/or team scores can be made a small part of their grades; or, if the school gives separate grades for effort, these scores can be used to determine the effort grades.

Figure 11. Bumping

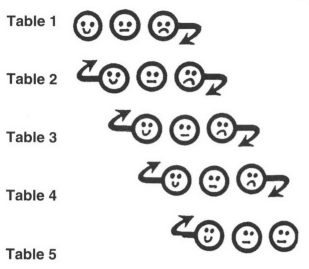

BUMPING

Table 1

Table 2

Table 3

Table 4

Table 5

Figure 12. Sample Tournament Table Assignment Sheet with Bumping (TGT)

Tournament Table Assignment Sheet   **(five tournament tables)**

Tournament number

Student	Team	1	2	3	4	5	6	7	8	9	10	11	12	13
Sam	Orioles	1	1	2										
Sarah	Cougars	1	2	2										
Tyrone	Whiz Kids	①	①	1										
Maria	Geniuses	②	1	1										
Liz	Orioles	2	②	1										
John T.	Cougars	2	③	2										
Sylvia	Whiz Kids	3	3	4										
Tom	Geniuses	③	2	3										
John F.	Orioles	3	4	5										
Tanya	Whiz Kids	4	④	3										
Carla	Orioles	④	3	3										
Kim	Cougars	4	5	5										
Carlos	Geniuses	4	4	4										
Shirley	Whiz Kids	5	5	5										
Ralph	Cougars	⑤	4	4										
Ruth	Geniuses	5	⑤	4										

NOTE:

③ indicates *high* scorer at Table 3

3 indicates *middle* scorer at Table 3

<u>3</u> indicates *low* scorer at Table 3

Results of most recent tournament

Tournament table assignment for next tournament

JIGSAW STRATEGY

In this section a procedure for structuring cooperative learning groups called **Jigsaw** is described. Each group member will be given a different section of the material to be learned. Each member is dependent on the others for information to do well on the assignment. Each group member is accountable for teaching his or her information to the other group members and learning the information they are teaching. The purposes of the jigsaw strategy are to:

1. Provide an alternative method of introducing new materials besides reading and lecture.

2. Create information interdependence among participants to increase their sense of mutuality.

3. Ensure that participants orally re hearse and cognitively elaborate the information being learned.

4. Model a cooperatively structured lesson.

Cooperative Triads

Join a triad heterogeneous on the basis of subject area and grade level taught. Your task is to learn all the assigned material. Work cooperatively to ensure that all group members master all the assigned material.

Preparation To Teach By Pairs

Take one section of the material and find a member of another group who has the same section of the material as you do. Work cooperatively to complete these tasks:

1. Learn and become an expert on your material. Read the material together, discuss it, and master it. Use the Search and Explain Procedure:

    a. Both persons silently read a paragraph. Person A summarizes the content to Person B.

    b. Person B listens, checks for accuracy, and states how it relates to material previously learned.

    c. The two reverse roles and repeat the procedure.

2. Plan how to teach your material to the other group members. Share your ideas as to how best to teach the material. Make sure your partner is ready.

    a. As you read through the material, underline the important points, write questions or ideas in the margins, and add your own thoughts and suggestions.

    b. When finished, write down the major ideas and supporting details or examples.

    c. Prepare one or more visual aids to help you explain the material.

    d. Plan how to make the other members of your group intellectually active rather than passive while they listen to your presentation.

Practicing How To Teach In Pairs

Meet with another person who is from a different group but who prepared to teach the same section of the material as you did. Work cooperatively to complete these tasks:

1. Review what each person plans to teach his/her group and share ideas on how to teach the material. Incorporate the best ideas from both plans into each person's presentation.

2. Make sure the other person is ready to teach the material.

Cooperative Triads

Meet with your original triad and complete the cooperative task of ensuring that all triad members have mastered all the assigned material by:

1. Teaching your area of expertise to the other triad members.

2. Learning the material being taught by the other triad members.

The presenter should encourage:

1. Oral rehearsal
2. Elaboration and integration
3. Implementation ideas

The role of the listening members is to:

1. Clarify the material by asking appropriate questions.

2. Help the presenter by coming up with clever ways of memorizing the important ideas or facts. Think creatively about the information being presented.

3. Relate (out loud) the information to previous learned knowledge. Elaborate the information being presented.

4. Plan (out loud) how the information can be applied in the immediate future.

Monitoring of the Groups

The instructor monitors each group to make sure that what is being taught is accurate. Collect some data about the functioning of the triads to aid their later group processing.

Evaluating

The instructor assesses participants' mastery of all the material by giving every participant a written exam or randomly giving individual oral exams on the material being studied.

Processing

The instructor has the cooperative triads process briefly by identifying at least one action each member did to help the other members learn and at least three actions that could be added to improve members' learning next time.

References

Johnson, D.W. & Johnson, R.T. (1988). Cooperation in the classroom. Edina, MN: Interaction Book Company.

Johnson, D.W. & Johnson, R.T. (1991). In Waxman/Walbert (1990). Effective teaching: Current research. Berkely, CA: McCutchan Publishing Company.

Slavin, R.E. (1986). Using student team learning. Baltimore, MD: Johns Hopkins University.

The results of a group's study often are presented in a skit or a song.

Chapter Three
Developing the Skills Needed for Cooperative Learning

The Cooperative and Collaborative Skills

Anyone who has worked with young adolescents knows the importance of guiding social development. Parents grow watchful as their children move toward the end of elementary education knowing that major changes will come with the transition from childhood to adolescence. Many terms have been used to describe 10-14 year olds—transescents, preadolescents, early adolescents, and others A child may experience a smooth, gradual, and relatively serene transition from childhood or may experience tantrums, tears, and trauma. It's hard to predict the emotional climate that will surround a given child's entry into adolescence.

The importance placed on social skills is expanding. Most people realize that a college degree or specialized vocational training alone is not enough to assure success in our world today. Employers value good interpersonal skills, competence in verbal communication, the ability to make decisions, and initiative. A prime question in the mind of any employer when interviewing applicants for a position is: Can this person get along with other people? Technical competence is not enough to ensure a successful career. While many social skills are learned in family and community experiences, contemporary children and adolescents often lack basic social skills. Students need to learn the importance of effectively communicating, building and maintaining trust, providing leadership, and managing conflicts. Yet, the schools have restricted student-to-student interaction. Therefore, students who have never been taught to work collaboratively will lack the needed social skills and find themselves alienated, isolated, and in poor mental health.

One of the great advantages of cooperative learning is that important "life survival" skills can be mastered within a task-structured classroom environment. The development of good social skills is really a prerequisite for achieving academic skills, since achievement improves as students become more effective in working with and learning from each other.

Teaching Cooperative Skills

According to Johnson, Johnson, and Holubec (1988), there are four assumptions underlying the teaching of cooperative skills to students. The first is that prior to teaching the skills a cooperative classroom environment must be established. An effective teacher will make students aware of the need for collaboration by the atmosphere created. It is important to establish a feeling tone within the group that students must "sink or swim together" and be involved in enhancing their own learning and the learning of their group-mates.

Second, cooperative skills have to be taught. Children are not born instinctively knowing how to cooperate with others. Teachers who have failed in cooperative learning are usually those who have tried to introduce cooperative learning without attention to the feeling tone of the classroom and the teaching of collaborative skills. Learning how to interact with others is no different from learning the basic skills associated with math, science, social studies, or language arts.

Third, while it is the teacher who structures cooperation within the classroom and initially defines the skills required to collaborate, the other group members largely determine whether the skills are learned and internalized. Peer support, peer feedback, and the processing of group work

are the responsibilities of the group. Students who learn to monitor their behavior and reflect upon their effectiveness in working with a group will develop social skills that will stand them in good stead both in school and in life.

The fourth assumption is that the earlier students are taught cooperative skills, the better. Students who begin practicing cooperative skills in the elementary grades will have a good foundation in collaborative working relationships. Their skills can be enhanced in the middle grades if these early competencies are reinforced and extended as the maturation process unfolds. To inform adults already on the job about how to cooperate more effectively with others is a little late. According to Johnson, Johnson, and Holubec (1988), "There is a direct relation between schools demanding that students work alone without interacting with each other and the number of adults in our society who lack the competencies required to work effectively with others in career, family, and leisure settings" (p. 5:4).

How does a teacher decide which cooperative social skills to teach? Which skills can be learned formally and which ones informally? The answers to such questions depend upon the cooperative skill level that already exists in the classroom. Students who have practiced collaborative and cooperative skills in prior grades may enter the middle school with a sense of these competencies and would need less time on the basics of forming the group and norming the group. The more sophisticated social skills would then be the focus for such individuals.

Some of the cooperative and collaborative skills associated with positive group relationships that are appropriate at the middle level are these:
- encouraging others
- praising good ideas
- describing feelings
- paraphrasing
- expressing support to the group
- directing the group's work
- listening to each other
- being "with it"
- being positive

How To Teach Cooperative Skills

Many educators believe that teaching cooperative skills to students is almost as important as teaching concepts in the basic subjects. And students are not *magically* going to work together successfully in a classroom without giving attention to the development of cooperative and collaborative skills.

The kind of learning required for successful group work is procedural learning. It is no different from playing golf or tennis, working on a car, or riding a bicycle. It differs from learning facts because it relies heavily on feedback and experimentation. The learner must modify performance and implementation until the errors are eliminated. The process is not automatic, it is gradual. Trial and error, and sometimes failure, are parts of the learning process. Success is guaranteed only with practice. Once the process is ingrained adequately students will perform without having to think about it.

Learning a cooperative skill results from a process of:

1. engaging in the skill,

2. obtaining feedback,

3. reflecting on the feedback,

4. modifying one's enactment and engaging in the skill again,

5. repeating steps 2, 3, and 4 again and again until the skill is appropriately used in a more automated fashion.

The performance of the learners is based upon their willingness to trust each other and talk frankly about one another's behavior. Expertise cannot be obtained unless students are willing to recognize each other's lack of expertise. The teacher must monitor the performance of the group and identify the students who are having difficulty. Students ultimately not only obtain a valuable set of skills for life but are likely to raise their achievement as well.

Group Dynamics

When individuals are asked to cooperate as a group, a natural progression occurs between and among group members. The process can be divided into various levels often characterized as *forming, norming, storming,* and *performing.* At each of the stages, the group dynamics and expectations are different. In the *forming* stage, the cooperative skills that need to be learned are the initial set of management skills directed toward organizing the group. This may mean something as simple as moving desks together without undue noise and commotion, to using quiet voices and encouraging others to participate. The success of these early interactions are often dependent upon the teacher's ability to set a positive classroom environment and to have already in place an effective management system.

The second level is the *norming* stage which involves the groups's effort to complete their tasks and maintain effective working relationships among members. Cooperative skills needed may include giving direction, expressing support and acceptance, asking for help, paraphrasing, energizing, and describing one's feelings. Fostering a positive work atmosphere and keeping the students on task is vital for effective leadership in cooperative learning groups.

The third level, *storming,* is inevitable. If honest appraisal and feedback are encouraged among group members an initial loss of identity and individuality occurs. As groups enter into this phase of the group process cycle, group members often assert themselves, both positively and negatively, or they look for a niche in the group. Some students may be a clown in their group; others may be the cynic. Whatever form the group takes, the storming is easily recognized by both the teacher and the students themselves as group members search for their special identity while developing a group personality. Knowing that the storming stage will occur, you can talk to the students about it. Let them know that storming means progress is being made toward developing a more cooperative and effective group. Until storming occurs the group's work is probably somewhat superficial. On the surface, everyone may be polite and accommodating, much like we are with "company," but not ready to tackle serious work. As members begin to know one another, they sense the various viewpoints, motives and persuasions among themselves. While each one feels a need to assert himself/herself as an individual within the group, a commonality begins to emerge. Encourage your students to celebrate this time of change within the group. Hold a class meeting and talk about the transition that is occurring. After the storming has been publicly noted and properly celebrated through open discussion and appropriate action, the power of the groups can be harnessed.

The next natural progression is to move toward a dynamic model of interaction that propels the group to the *performance stage.* As students acquire the skills for critical and creative thinking, they also turn inward and begin feeling better about themselves. No longer is there a need to be a show-off, class clown, or cynic in a group. Members begin to realize the importance of each contribution and value each other's intellect. When this occurs members are ready to consider positively the feelings, concerns, and suggestions of others.

In this last stage of performance teachers can carefully structure the cognitive tasks and match each with a collaborative and cooperative social skill so that high functioning, cooperative groups will result. When we help students learn in ways that hold them accountable and responsible for each and every group member and for achieving the task at hand, they will perform admirably.

Teachers trying cooperative learning in their classrooms must be patient, for it takes time to develop in their students the ability to work successfully in groups. Group dynamics is a process, not an entity. Open discussions about the stages and the problems will pay off. Allowing time for students to process their own work is valuable. While the initial task of organizing the group is the responsibility of the teacher, the real monitoring of the group's work must be done by the group.

How To Process in a Group

To be productive as individuals within a group structure group members must learn to *process.* Processing is aimed at providing accurate, non-threatening feedback concerning the procedures the group is using to achieve its out-

come goals. The feedback gives group members information that helps them improve performance. Group processing depends upon:

1. student to student interaction

2. use of observations to provide feedback to group members as individuals and to the group as a whole.

3. reflecting on feedback to identify problems the members have in functioning effectively.

4. planning how to be more effective the next time they work in groups.

Every learning experience is also a lesson in learning how to collaborate when the group members process how well their group has functioned. While considerable time and attention have been paid to structuring teams and organizing for interdisciplinary instruction, less attention has been focused on training students to promote the processing by group members of their collaborative efforts. Teachers must discuss what collaborative skills are being used and not used in the group and plan how they may improve their students' performance. A cognitive skill is matched with a collaborative or cooperative skill as group members learn group dynamics and interact effectively with each other. Sometimes processing will be quite brief and short, while at other times, it will be extensive and require more time. Either way, an integral part of group work should be having groups reflect on their effectiveness for these reasons.

1. If students are to learn the most from their experience in group work, they must reflect on that experience. Unexamined experience rarely benefits anyone.

2. Problems encountered in collaborating effectively may be prevented from recurring by group processing.

3. Systematic processing of group functioning promotes the development and use of the important cooperative skills.

4. When groups first begin to work together, They tend to be very task-oriented. Processing gives the groups the time they need to maintain effective working relationships. (Johnson, and Johnson, and Holubec, 1988 p. 6:3).

Procedures for Processing

There are two opportunities for providing time so that members can process how well they are collaborating. The first is to provide a few minutes at the end of each working session for immediate feedback. The second is to invite observers to watch the interaction of the group during a work session and then report on their observations. When groups are being formed at the beginning of the year, it is best to allow them to examine themselves and reflect on members' ability to work together. This helps emphasize the self-examination and reflection that are necessary for groups to be effective. It also gives opportunity to discuss the group process while it is fresh in the group's memory. After group members become used to processing and are proficient in using collaborative skills, processing sessions can them become intermittent, perhaps once or twice a semester, just to remind group members to stay focused on improving their collaborative skills.

Group member processing on an informal basis can be completed within the group in the following way. A prepared checklist or questionnaire could be used giving their impressions as to how well they or the group functioned. The focus of the questions could be what the member did (I,ME), what other members did (YOU,THEY), or what all members did (WE). After the group has completed the checklist following a planning session together, the group summarizes their perceptions. A sample checklist or STEM statement can be used. At the end of each work session the members share orally within the group their impressions. As the teacher monitors the group's interaction in a classroom, one of the following stems can be selected for each work session.

I observed.....

I liked the way.....

I saw.......

I heard......

I noticed......

Ask each group member to complete one of the following....

I appreciated it when you (we)......

I liked it when you (we)......

I admire it the way we are.....

I enjoy it when you (we).....

You really helped out the group when you.....

The group members need to reflect on and learn to analyze the group session they just completed in order to discover what helped and what hindered them in completing the day's work and whether specific behaviors had a positive or negative effect. Such reflection and analysis are generally structured by the group member assigned the role of *checker* or *encourager*.

If formal observation of the group's working relationship is desired by a visitor/observer, identify skills and behaviors to be emphasized and observed. Appoint observers and prepare an observation form for each. The group that is being observed can be informed of the collaborative expectations that are to be demonstrated. The observer then reports to the group the data gathered and group members discuss their impressions as to how they behaved. Group members reflect on and analyze the effectiveness of their behavior by comparing their observed behavior with their own impressions or expectations for their performance. Group members publicly set goals for performing collaborative skills in the next group session. The following formal observation sheet formats were adapted from Johnson, Johnson, and Holubec (1988).

The first one can be used by the teacher to record the general tenor of the several groups while they are at work. The second form would be used to record the actions of individuals in a particular group. The third form would be used to assess progress made by students following the teaching of a specific skill, while the last form would provide a long-term record of the progress of one group.

Observation Sheet 1:
Teacher Observing Groups

Groups	Explaining Concepts	Encouraging Participation	Checking Understanding	Organizing The Work
1				
2				
3				
4				
5				

Observation Sheet 2:
Intensive Observation

Actions	Student name	Student name	Student name	Student name
Encourages others to participate				
Explains concepts and principles				
Expresses support				
Gives direction				
Asks for information, rationale				
Paraphrases				

Add-on Observation Sheet

Start by teaching one skill and observing for it. Show students how well they do in practicing that skill; praise and otherwise reward their efforts. Whey they have mastered one skill, add and teach a second skill, etc.

Date _____   Period _____   Observer _____

Skills	Group Members			

OTHER OBSERVATION NOTES:

Long-Term Group Progress

Curriculum Unit _____

Group Members _____

Date	Added Ideas	Encouraged Others	Summarized/ Clarified	Finished Work	Asked for Help

Summary

This chapter began by explaining the importance of guiding the social development of the young adolescent. Cooperative learning and social skill strategies have been provided to meet this end. The matter of learning group processing, group dynamics, and related social skills is in itself a process. Students need procedural learning instruction to successfully work in groups, and time must be allowed for reflection so that group interaction can be enhanced.

References

Johnson, D.W., Johnson, R.T. & Holubec, E. (1988). *Cooperation in the classroom*. Edina, MN: Interaction Book Company.

Chapter Four
Putting Cooperative Learning into Action

Getting Started

Teachers will not become proficient in using cooperative learning simply by reading this book or by taking a workshop. Teachers, like all learners, become proficient from doing. Developing expertise in cooperative learning procedures requires conscious planning, thought, and practice. One of the most important contributions that you can make to your school is to support cooperation among teachers while encouraging the use of cooperative learning in the classroom. It is easier to establish cooperative learning in your own classroom if there is a sense of cooperation among all school personnel.

How do you encourage cooperation among teachers? The process is the same as for implementing cooperation among students. Establish cooperative goals that require interdependence and interaction among the teachers. If your teachers share common planning time, you are well on your way toward establishing shared decision-making, trust, and openness. In schools where feelings of hostility, alienation, guardedness, and anxiety are present, teacher creativity is stifled. Such school environments are depressing and discouraging. But in schools where a cooperative attitude is present, teachers feel enough trust to visit each other's classroom, ask one another for help or suggestions, and provide feedback about each other's teaching.

In order to implement cooperative learning procedures, the teacher must first try out the new instructional strategy. This means being willing to experiment. Such experimentation involves the risk of failure. According to Johnson, Johnson, and Holubec (1988), an attitude of experimentation means that teachers are willing to:

1. Believe that teaching is a continuous process of developing more effective procedures through modifying old procedures and integrating new ones into one's standard practices. The continuous improvement of teaching becomes both a personal and professional commitment.

2. Accept barriers and problems as a natural aspect of modifying teaching procedures (as opposed to believing they are proof that the new procedures will not work). Innovating always carries the risk of failure and of meeting problems and roadblocks. In highly innovative organizations there is a very high failure rate because new things are constantly being tried out.

3. View problems and roadblocks as signs that adjustments are needed in the implementation (as opposed to defeat or failure). Problems and roadblocks need to be viewed as temporary barriers rather than as permanent obstacles. Learning from one's mistakes is a talent found in teachers who continuously improve their teaching competence (p. 7:7).

Successfully implementing cooperative learning in the schools is heavily dependent upon the creation of collegial support groups. If your school utilizes interdisciplinary teaming, the structure necessary for support groups already exists. Frequent informal but professional discussions about cooperative learning in which information is shared, successes are celebrated, and problems analyzed are key activities of a support group.

Quick Cooperative Starters

The following cooperative learning starters use temporary, informal, or ad hoc groups that last from a few minutes to one class period.

They are often utilized so that students can engage in focused discussion before and after a brief lecture. These group ideas, dervied from Johnson, Johnson, and Holubec (1988), will help you get started.

1. Turn to Your Neighbor: Three to five minutes. Ask the student to turn to a neighbor and ask something about the lesson: to explain a concept you've just taught; to summarize the three most important points of the discussion, or whatever fits the lesson.

2. Reading Groups: Students read material together and answer the questions. One person is the Reader, another the Recorder, and the third the Checker (who checks to make certain everyone understands and agrees with the answers). They must come up with three possible answers to each question and circle their favorite one. When finished, they sign the paper to certify that they all understand and agree on the answers.

3. Jigsaw: Each person reads and studies part of a selection, then teaches what he or she has learned to the other members of the group. Each then quizzes the group members until satisfied that everyone knows his or her part thoroughly.

4. Focus Trios: Before a film, lecture, or reading, students identify what they already know about the subject and come up with questions they have about it. Afterwards, the trios answer questions, discuss new information, and formulate new questions.

5. Drill Partners: Students drill each other on the facts they need to know until they are certain both partners know and can remember them all. This works for spelling, vocabulary, math, grammar, test review, etc. Give bonus points on the test if all members score above a certain percentage.

6. Reading Buddies: Students read their stories to each other, getting help with words and discussing content with their partners. Students tell about their books and read their favorite parts to each other.

7. Homework Checkers: Students compare homework answers, discuss any they have not answered similarly, then correct their papers and add the reason they changed an answer. They make certain everyone's answers agree, then staple the papers together. You grade one paper from each group and give group members that grade.

8. Worksheet Checkmates: Two students, each with different jobs, complete one worksheet. The Reader reads, suggests an answer; the Writer agrees or comes up with another answer. When they both understand and agree on an answer, the Writer can record it.

9. Test Reviewers: Students prepare each other for a test. They get bonus points if every group member scores above a preset level.

10. Composition Pairs: Student A explains what she/he plans to write to Student B, while Student B takes notes or makes an outline. Together they plan the opening or thesis statement; then Student B explains while Student A writes. They exchange outlines, and use them in writing their papers.

11. Board Workers: Students go together to the chalkboard. One can be the Answer Suggester, one the Checker to see if everyone agrees, and one the Writer.

12. Problem Solvers: Groups are given a problem to solve. Each student must contribute to part of the solution. Groups can decide who does what, but they must show where all members contributed. Or they can decide together, but each must be able to explain how to solve the problem.

13. Computer Groups: Students work together on the computer. They must agree on the input before it is typed in. One person is the Keyboard Operator, another the Monitor Reader, a third the Verifier (who collects opinions on the input from the other two and makes the final decision). Roles are rotated daily so everyone gets experience at all three jobs.

14. Book Report Pairs: Students interview each other on the books they read, then they report on their partner's book.

15. Writing Response Groups: Students read and respond to each other's papers three times:

A: They mark what they like with a star and put a question mark anywhere there is some thing they didn't understand or think is weak. Then they discuss the paper as a whole with the writer.

B. They mark problems with grammar, usage, punctuation, spelling, or format and discuss it with the other.

C. They proofread the final draft and point out any errors for the author to correct. (Teachers can assign questions for students to answer about their group members' papers to help them focus on certain problems or skills.)

16. Skill Teachers/Concept Clarifiers: Students work with each other on skills (like identifying adjectives in sentences or showing proof in algebra) and/or concepts (like "ecology" or "economics") until both can do or explain them easily.

17. Summary Pairs: Students alternate reading and orally summarizing paragraphs. One reads and summarizes while the other checks the paragraph for accuracy and adds anything left out. They alternate roles with each paragraph.

18. Elaborating and Relating Pairs: Students elaborate on what they are reading and learning, relating it to what they already know about the subject. This can be done before and after reading a selection, listening to a lecture, or seeing a film.

19. Group Reports: Students research a topic together. Each one is responsible for checking at least one different source and writing at least three notecards of information. They write the report together; each person is responsible for seeing that his/her information is included. For oral reports, each must take a part and help each other rehearse until they are all at ease.

20. Playwrights: Students write a play together, perhaps about a time period recently studied—then practice and perform it for the class.

What do I do with the student who . . .

Even the most skilled teachers will encounter a student who will not cooperate as a part of a group. In most cases, the student may lack social skills. Even if all the strategies previously given are in place, it is unreal to assume that every child, every day, and in every situation can maintain perfect cooperation. So here are some suggestions for working with the most troubled child.

Whatever the misbehavior, it is important to have a two stage response—*timeout* and *goal redirection*. In both stages, the critical ingredient is knowing how to nurture the student's responsibility to control his/her behavior.

STAGE 1: TIMEOUT

To enhance self-responsibility of students in the cooperative classroom, introduce and use timeout places. One timeout place may be in the classroom and the other may be near the principal's office. Timeout works best if the students can elect to use the timeout when they want to. However, it is important to specify appropriate timeout activity. The teacher should not permit the student to sit and do nothing. If the student elects to use the timeout place, then regulate the type of activity that can be completed during the timeout. In the beginning, the timeout place may be crowded, other days, it may be empty. Students who elect timeout also elect "timein" when they feel ready to rejoin the group. For the most part, it is important that the student recognize he/she is the decision maker in control of timeouts and timeins. It may be a good idea to have paper and a clip board handy so students can record the frequency of the timeout place. For younger children 15 minute limit should suffice, for older students, 40 minutes should be the maximum. Whatever the reason, the most important thing is to encourage students to make wise choices.

It is a right to learn. It is a privilege to learn in a group.
—Blueprints for Thinking in the Cooperative Classroom, 1990.

If a student is excluded from the group, two guidelines apply. First, the student must finish the assignment alone. The group reorganizes itself to work without the offender. Second, the offender must convince the group that he/she is ready to rejoin the group. If the group votes the offender out, the offender must contract with the group for his/her return. For return to the group, several conditions must be met:

• The student must describe his/her misbehavior that leads to timeout.

• The student must contract how he/she will behave differently, assuring positive contributions (preferably in writing).

The student who disrupts the group, should not be allowed to return to the group mid-task. Separation from the group means for the entire time the group is engaged on that day in that period.

Teacher observation should be the basis for separating a student from the group rather than from student's report. Monitoring the classroom as a facilitator for student learning is the preferred teacher style. When it is beyond the group's ability to handle it, step in and address the situation.

STRATEGY # 1: The Tell ME strategy from *Blueprints for Thinking in the Cooperative Classroom* is helpful.

"(Student's name), tell me what you are doing." –

(There are a variety of answers possible—"Nothing." "They made me"; or "I was_____." If the answer is "Nothing," try humor, "Only dead people do nothing. Are you dead?" or identify the behavior, "I saw you _____. Was I seeing visions?"

Next ask, "What is your role? In that role, what are you supposed to do?" (If you have set up the groups carefully, the answer should be quick. If the student says, "I don't know" give him/her a timeout to think it over, to read the role bulletin board or to ask someone else in the group. Insist that the student tell you the expected job.)

Third, ask, "How is what you were doing helping you do your assigned job?" (This question may evoke silence or a creative answer with which you must disagree.)

Finally, ask the student to decide on a new behavior. "Are you ready to (expected behavior)?"

If the answer is "no," give the student timeout to complete the group task alone. If the student says "yes," then indicate that he/she may return to the group only if the new behavior is used. As soon as the misbehavior reoccurs, the student takes timeout. Outline the conditions for return: (a) "When we can agree how you will behave," and (b)

"you show it." Monitor the student's behavior after he/she returns to the group. Acknowledge with special recognition the new positive behavior.

STRATEGY # 2: Constructing a T-Chart may be useful if the social skills needed are lacking among an individual or a group. This strategy was taken from *Cooperation in the Classroom*.

CONSTRUCTING A T-CHART

1. Write the name of the skill to be learned and practiced and draw a large T underneath.

2. Title the left side of the T "Looks Like" and the right side of the T "Sounds Like."

3. On the left side write a number of behaviors that operationalize the skill. One the right side write a number of phrases that operationalize the skill.

4. Have all the students practice "looks like" and "sounds like" several time before the lesson is conducted.

ENCOURAGING

LOOKS LIKE	SOUNDS LIKE
Thumbs up	"What is your idea?"
Pat on back	"I had not thought of that"
Shake hands	"Good idea!"
Nodding head	"That's interesting"

Other possible cooperative or collaborative skills associated with positive group relationships might include the following:
• praising each other
• describing feeling
• paraphrasing
• expressing support to group
• giving direction to group's work
• listening to each other
• being with it
• being positive

STAGE II: WHAT NEXT?

Working with the middle school student who does not want to cooperate may present a challenge. When "timeout" doesn't work for a certain student, what is your recourse?

Don't panic. Concentrate the bulk of the energy (80%) on improving the cooperative skills of the cooperative students. (Out-of-control classrooms usually result when a teacher's energy is focused on the 5-8% of the students who try to disrupt any class.)

Be persistent. The students who don't cooperate, probably can't. It is not likely that behaviors or attitudes will change overnight. More likely, these students have had years of reinforcement for their misbehavior patterns. Solid doses of patience and persistence are needed to see even the first glimmer of change.

Plan a strategy. Behavior change takes time. Attitude change takes more time, and personal value change takes the most time. Reduce the time and increase the impact with a strategic plan to help the reluctant student discover the personal benefits of cooperation.There is no *recipe* for promoting changes. However, to know in advance how to deal with the predictable possibilities for disruption will help the success barometer to rise.

Teach signals. For creating order in a cooperative learning classroom use the following teaching signal for getting students attention. This signal can be used with any group. Sometimes it is more difficult to get students in a group to stop working than it is to get them in a group. Shouting above their concentrated conversation turns any teacher's voice sour. Relying on a practiced signal is essential for the cooperative classroom.

For the most effective signal, use the well-proven "hands up" which can be used with any age group.

Introduce the signal by explaining what it's for.

"I'll hold up my hand when everyone should stop talking and pay attention to me."

This signal alerts them to listen for the next set of instructions. Invite the students to do three things when they see the teacher's hand up: (1) complete their thoughts, (2) put up their hands, and (3) look at the teacher without talking. When all are silent and looking at the teacher, praise their attention ("I appreciate your prompt cooperation.") and give the next instruction.

After explaining the signal, then practice. Use wait time, supported by eye contact. If some students persist in talking while others have their hands up, use "proximity"—move next to the laggards and stand there with a raised hand.

"Remember, when the hand goes up, the mouth goes closed."

There are several appropriate times to use the signal. Here are the three most common uses of the signal: (1) when giving class instructions, (2) when class talk becomes too loud and controlled voice levels (i.e. 3" 6" 12" voices) are needed, and (3) when a student or guest is to address the class. If all teachers in the school use the same signal, students benefit all the more. But it is not necessary that every teacher use the same signal. Some prefer to flick the lights, ring a bell, or use the hand T signal for timeout. Any signal is fine as long as it is taught, practiced, and used consistently.

SUMMARY

This chapter presented an overview of some strategies that can assist with the cooperative classroom learning process. A number of management strategies were given.

Cooperative learning is not a cure for poor classroom management. A middle school teacher with poor management skills will still have poor discipline with cooperative learning. Good classroom management is a prerequisite to the cooperative classroom. On the other hand, the teacher who has good management skills can, with reasonable persistence and patience, take students to a higher level of learning in which they are thinkers, workers, and proud achievers.

References

Johnson, D.W., Johnson, R.T. & Holubec, E. (1988). *Cooperation in the classroom*. Edina, MN: Interaction Book Company.

Fogarty, R. and Bellanca, J. (1990). *Blueprints for thinking in the cooperative classroom*. Skylight Publishers Inc.

Part II
Lesson Strategies

Students become teachers in cooperative learning—and learn well in the process.

PART II

This part is a compilation of lesson strategies that have been tried in middle school classrooms. Most lessons are topical in nature and are organized by content areas. The individual lesson format fits the style or classroom situation of the teacher that developed it. Different teachers, for example, structured positive interdependence in various ways. Some did it through bonus points, some through divisions of working roles, some through jigsawing materials, and some through group grades.

The following lessons may be and should be adapted to a teacher's style, personality, students, and school. Lasting implementation requires that teachers "reinvent" the teaching practices for themselves. Some lessons deal only with the acquisition of specific information while others bring problem-solving skills into play. Many indicate a particular grade level but most are adaptable to other grades. These lessons were developed by different individuals but can be revised for use in your classroom. Glancing through them all will give you a "feel" for cooperative learning as it can be practiced, both in its simplest forms and in its more complex procedures.

The following basic elements are provided in almost all of these lessons.

1. A description of the lesson to be taught and the expected learning outcome.

2. A clear description of the procedures:

   a. group size, composition, distribution of materials.

   b. positive interdependence, task, individual accountability.

   c. monitoring procedures.

   d. group processing procedures.

3. The materials necessary to conduct the lesson.

These lesson strategies are sources of ideas for making your own lessons or in many cases can be used as is. Either way, you'll find them of value as you launch into cooperative learning.

Art

Students' attitudes toward education show improvement when cooperative learning is used.

A PICTURE SAYS A THOUSAND WORDS

by
Katherine McGhee

Grade: 6, 7, and/or 8

Content: Art and Creative Writing

Group Size: Teams of five

Assigned Roles: Reader, Recorder, Observer, Checker, Encourager

Materials: An assortment of color art reproductions in a variety of subjects, pencils, and paper.

Set: Divide students into groups of five. They will work at desks arranged in a circle or on the floor. Distribute one envelope of color art reproductions* to each group. Students will be instructed not to open the envelope until directed.

Objective: Working cooperatively, students will write a story using color reproductions as the motivating agent.

Task: After each group has received their envelope of colored art reproductions, they will be instructed to open them. Then they will arrange the three reproductions in any order and place them on a table or the floor in front of them. Students will then have the task of writing a story using the reproductions as a motivator. The first picture will be the beginning of the story, the second picture will be the middle of the story, and the third picture will be the end of the story. The more unrelated the reproductions are, the more challenging the task is to tie them together in a story format. Each person in the group will have an assigned task:

- Recorder   This person will do all of the writing as the group dictates the story.

- Observer   This person will closely scrutinize the art reproduction help to write the story according to what is observed.

- Checker   This person will make sure the story has a beginning, a middle and an end and that it corresponds to the art reproductions.

and

- Encourager   This person will help to keep everyone on task.

- Reader   This person will read the story to the rest of the class.

Processing: Using the stem statement after the activity of "We could do better at..."

Closure: After each group has completed their story, the reader from each will share the stories with the rest of the class. The art reproductions used will be shared as well. There will then be a discussion of the lessons learned from each person performing a specific role.

*Art reproductions can be postcard size and could be purchased at any art museum gift shop or bookstore. Old calendars with art reproductions can serve for this activity as well. Inexpensive color reproductions (postcard size) can also be purchased through University Prints.

CLASSICAL COLUMNS

by
Katherine McGhee

Grade:	6, 7 or 8
Content:	Art
Group Size:	Teams of six
Assigned Roles:	Client, Architect, Three Building Contractors, Encourager
Materials:	Large cardboard rolls from carpeting or paper, white poster board scraps, scissors, glue, tempera paints, brushes, and visuals of various types of columns, i.e. Corinthian, Doric and Ionic. Some suggestions would be the Greek Parthenon and the Roman Coliseum. Cards with Corinthian, Doric and Ionic columns on them.
Objective:	Working cooperatively, students will produce two like columns (either Doric, Ionic or Corinthian) for a doorway entrance.

Task:

Pass out cards with column illustrations on them. Those with Corinthian columns will form one group, those with Doric columns will form another group and those with Ionic columns will form the third group. Look at illustrations or slides of the various column styles and have students note the similarities and differences. For example, the Corinthian and Ionic columns are more ornate compared to the Doric style.

The different parts of the column should be discussed as well by using the accompanying illustrations. Students can then take a field trip around town to identify the different kinds of columns utilized in modern architecture.

Members of the group will then choose a role to play for the art project.
- Client: Describes the kind of columns to be constructed for some entrance-way within the school.
- Architect: Develops the design for the columns to meet the client's needs.
- Contractors: Do the construction of the columns.
- Encourager: Helps to keep the group on task.

Once the roles have been established, an entrance-way within the school will be selected. The client and the architect will work closely in arriving at a suitable design. Those in the Corinthian group will design a modern version of a Corinthian column and those in the Doric and Ionic groups will design their columns likewise.

The contractors will build the columns according to the specifications of the architect and client. Columns can be constructed out of large cardboard rolls from carpeting or newsprint from the local newspaper. They can be painted and embellished by folding and cutting poster board into various designs and gluing them onto the column.

Processing:	Using the stem statement after each activity of "We could do better at..."
Closure:	Once the columns are completed, they can be attached by tape or a hot glue gun to the wall that surrounds either side of the entrance-way. The creations can then be shared with the rest of the class. As a group, the students will decide if the column designs fall into their respective categories, Corinthian, Doric and Ionic.

PEOPLE AS ART OBJECTS
by
Katherine McGhee

Grade: 6, 7, or 8

Content: Art

Group Size: Teams of five

Group Assignments: Use cards with ethnic headdresses, facial adornment and body fashions. Pass them out.

Materials: Slides of ethnic dress from Africa, i.e. the Berbers, the Masai. Slides should show same people as on the cards that are passed out at the beginning of class. Also needed are: glue, tempera paint in assorted colors, scissors, tissue paper in various colors, face paint, crepe paper in various colors, fabric scraps, assorted beads, sequins, buttons, feathers, yarn in a variety of colors, and string. The book entitled, "Africa Adorned" by Angela Fisher, Harry Abrams, Inc. 1984, is a good reference.

Set: Show slides of people from various cultures in Africa wearing their traditional dress. Encourage students to discuss the similarities and differences of these articles of clothing.

Objective: Students will learn about the dress of various cultures as well as learning to work cooperatively.

Task: After viewing slides of ethnic dress from various cultures, the cooperative phase will begin. Students who have cards of headdresses will form one group, those with facial adornment will form another group, and those with body adornment will form the third group. Within each group will be: a **Reader,** whose job it will be to further investigate headdresses, facial adornments or body adornment from different cultures. Their job will entail going to the library and providing the necessary reference books; a **Creator,** whose job it will be to make a headdress, facial adornment, or body adornment with a variety of materials provided by a teacher; a **Model,** whose job it will be to wear the headdress, facial adornment or body adornment; an **Encourager,** whose job it will be to keep the momentum of work going on in each group; an **Announcer,** whose job it will be to inform the class about the culture represented by the headdress, facial adornment or body adornment.

Student groups will make the art form indicated on their card. Those with headdresses will make a headdress, etc. A culture and the traditional dress will be chosen by the group. It will be researched. Then, a headdress, facial or body adornment will be designed in the spirit of the culture chosen. This means that the fashion designed does not have to exactly replicate what is found in the chosen culture, but can have a modern twist to it. For example, most traditional people use earth tones for color (reds, yellows, browns, etc.). These colors can be substituted with neon ones.

Processing: Using the stem statement after each activity of "We could do better at..."

Closure: Once the fashion is designed, each group will have the opportunity to present their creations to the class with the Announcer from each group providing background information on the costume presented. A discussion about the lessons learned from each person performing a specific role will take place as well.

PORTRAIT TOTEMS

by
Katherine McGhee

Grade:	7, 8, or 9
Content:	Art
Group Size:	Teams of five
Assigned Roles:	Designer, Sculptor, Painter, Assembler, Encourager
Materials:	Large boxes (in various sizes) suitable for stacking, plaster gauze (from medical supply stores), petroleum jelly, old buckets, access to water, old newspaper, drinking straws, shower caps, tempera paints, brushes, assorted construction paper, scissors, glue, feathers, fabric scraps, pipe cleaners, cardboard scraps, and visuals of Totem Poles by the Kwakuitl people, video: "Richard's Totem Pole" (distributed by Coronet Film and Video, 1981.)
Objective:	Working cooperatively, students will build a group totem utilizing their own self portraits.
Task:	Show a variety of visual examples of totem poles by the Kwakuitl people from the North Coast. These poles are placed outside their homes. They are carved symbols (a coat of arms) on wooden poles that tell the story of the family's origin. Most totems have a variety of faces (ancestors) on them. The video entitled, "Richard's Totem Pole" can be shown to further enhance the understanding of this art form. After this introduction, students will be divided into groups and given the following tasks.

Designer

This person will draw a sketch of what the final totem will look like using a variety of box sizes to assemble their totems. The totem will be sketched and suggested colors and patterns will be proposed by the designer.

Sculptor

This person will be in charge of making plaster casts of everyone's face in the group. Each person must cover his/her face with petroleum jelly and wear a shower cap. This will protect the face and hair. Plaster gauze strips (those used for casts on broken appendages) will then be cut into approximately six inch strips and soaked in warm water for a few minutes. Drinking straws will then be placed in the nostrils of each person to aid in breathing during the casting process. Now the sculptor can lay strips of the soaked gauze over the face, being careful to mold it to the curves and smoothing it out to prevent wrinkling. The whole face should be covered with at least three layers of gauze and then allowed to dry. The drying process only takes a few minutes and when the plaster is hard, the cast will easily slip off by carefully lifting it.

Assembler

This person will be in charge of adhering the portrait casts onto the surface of a box. There should be one face per box. These faces can be adhered with a low temperature glue gun or masking tape. Then the boxes can be stacked according to the Designer's specifications. At this point, the Assembler along with the Designer can add sculptural detail with cardboard, i.e. wing-like extensions, geometric headdresses, etc. Feathers and fabric scraps can be added as well. The totem can range from five to eight feet in height depending on the boxes utilized.

Painter

The painter will be in charge of mixing and preparing the paint supplies. This person, with the assistance of the designer and assembler, will paint the totem according to the specified plan.

Encourager

This person will motivate the group to complete the project and provide technical assistance when needed.

Processing: Using the stem statement after each activity of "We can do better at..."

Closure: Once the totems have been completed, each group can discuss if the designer's plan was adhered to. Totems can then be shared with the rest of the class and put on display in the school library or cafeteria.

SURREALISM

by
Katherine McGhee

Grade:	6, 7 or 8
Content:	Art
Group Size:	Teams of five
Assigned Roles:	Four illustrators, one encourager
Materials:	Prints of Salvadore Dali's Surrealistic works, i.e. "The Steps of Summer." Also needed will be 12"x18" white drawing paper and colored pencils or markers.
Objective:	Students will collaborate on a group figure drawing.

Task:

Time should be spent on a short discussion of what surrealism means. (This art movement began in the 1930s that extolled the virtues of the irrational by exploring the subconscious and casting new light on the depths of the soul. These were psychological documents whose total effect was strange and full of abnormalities, i.e. Dali's melting clocks.) Time should then be spent on looking at examples of Surrealist art by Salvador Dali and Renee Magritte.

Students will then be divided into groups of five. Each group will have one piece of drawing paper and colored pencils or markers. The paper will then be folded into four even sections width-wise. The first member of the group will draw a head on the top section which will then be folded over so that the next person cannot see what was drawn; the next member will draw a torso and fold this over so that the next person cannot see; the third member will draw the legs and fold it so the next person cannot see; and the fourth person will draw the feet. The fifth person will encourage all group members to participate.

Once the drawing is complete, it can be unfolded to reveal all of the parts. See accompanying illustrations.

Processing:

Using the stem statement after the activity of "We could do better at..."

Closure:

Each group will share their drawings and discuss how they worked together to achieve their results.

Mathematics

Many group activities require collaboration as in solving a tangram.

DOMINO MATH
by
Lisa M. Phillips

Grade: Six through eight (depending on the skill being taught)

Time: 20-30 minutes

Group Size: Two to four individuals

Group Assignment: After choosing group size, put one colored domino in a bag for each individual to be in that group.

Materials: Each group will need one set of dominoes, one pencil, and one assignment sheet.

Academic Task: Each group will be given one sheet to solve together. They will also be given one set of dominoes and one pencil to write down the solution. The assignment is to solve the problems correctly with only the dominoes shown.

Criteria for Success: Success will be determined if all group members can solve the problems correctly.

Positive Interdependence:

Each member of the group will be able to share their theories about how to accomplish the task with all members.

Individual Accountability:

When completed, I will call on one individual at random, from each group to show their solution on the overhead.

Expected Behaviors:

I expect to see the following things as I observe the groups:
- all students getting a chance to share their ideas
- encouraging by all individuals
- dominoes being used only for the task at hand

Monitoring: By teacher

Processing: The instructor will give positive reinforcement to both the individuals and groups. Instructor will ask for feedback about the behaviors and theories which were used to accomplish the task.

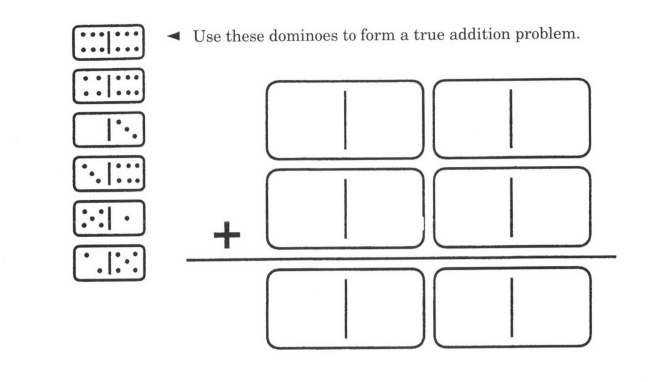

◄ Use these dominoes to form a true addition problem.

$+$

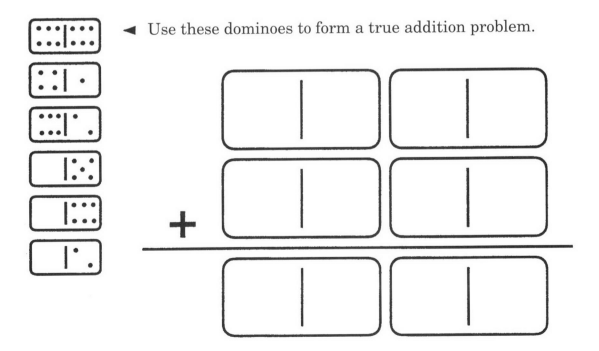

◄ Use these dominoes to form a true addition problem.

$+$

DOMINO MATH PROBLEM-SOLVING ACTIVITIES
1988 Creative Publications

Double-Six Dominoes

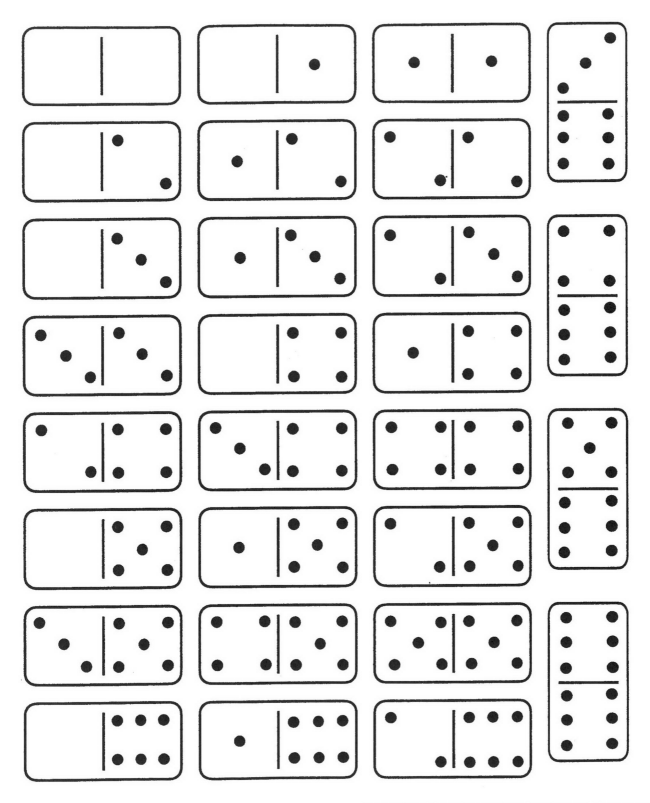

DOMINO MATH PROBLEM-SOLVING ACTIVITIES
1988 Creative Publications

Use 21 dominoes to cover the spaces. Do not use any domino with 6 dots on a side.
Make 3 sums of 215.

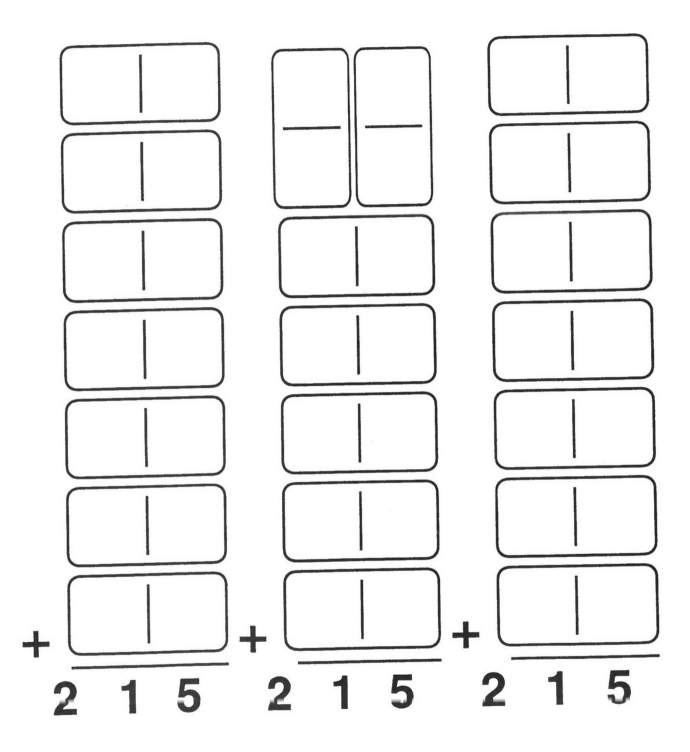

FOURS CHALLENGE
by
Norman Goethe

I. Decisions

Time Required:	30-40 Minutes
Grade Level:	6
Subject Area:	Math
Group Size:	Three individuals per group with the possibility of one group of four.
Group Assignments:	Students will count off by seven to form groups of three, and one group of four. Students will then count off by three in group to determine roles.

Roles:	Definitions:
Encourager:	Ensures everyone has an opportunity to share ideas, particularly the shy student.
Checker:	Makes sure all group members understand how to explain each answer.
Recorder:	Records the group's solution on the chart.

Materials:	Each group will need a piece of large white construction paper, markers, scratch paper, and pencils.

II. Set the Lesson

Academic Task: Each group must find ways to make as many numbers from one to twenty as you can, using only fours. You can use as many fours as you want, and any combination of addition, subtraction, multiplication, and division. For example, you could make the number two this way: $(4+4) \div 4 = 2$. Make a chart to show your methods. If you find more than one way for the same number put those ways in the chart also.

Criteria for Success: Success will be determined by each group's ability to complete the chart of all 20 numbers.

100% *Fantastic*	90% *Very Good*	80% *Good*

Positive Interdependence: Each member will be able to share ideas as to the methods used to solve each of the 20 answers. Each group will have members take turns sharing ideas and each member will be responsible for knowing the method for finding the answer.

Individual Accountability: Every member must be able to demonstrate the method of finding each respective answer of 1-20.

Expected Behaviors: I expect to see the following things when I observe the groups:
- using quiet voices.
- everyone having opportunity to share ideas.
- encouraging.
- praising.

III. Monitoring: Will be done by the teacher.

Focus will be on: individuals and individual groups.

Observation sheet includes the behaviors of: using quiet voices, everyone having an opportunity to share ideas, encouraging, and praising.

IV. Processing/Feedback: The teacher will move around the room providing reinforcement to individuals and groups. The teacher will chart the observable behaviors. The positive behaviors will be pointed out. Key ideas or "tricks" to solving the 20 answers will be explained by students.

GEOMETRIC SHAPES
by
Sue Mack

Grade Level: 7

Subject Area: Math

Step 1. Select a Lesson

Complete perimeter, triangle, and polygon worksheets to review comprehension of these geometric concepts.

Step 2. Make Decisions

a. Group size: Three
b. Assignment to groups: Count off heterogeneously by three.
c. Room arrangement: Tables in room are conducive to eye-to-eye contact
d. Materials needed for each group: two worksheets (one set per group). Students use geometry notebooks each has completed.
e. Assigning roles: Reader: Reads problem aloud. Checker: Checks to see all have notebooks. Recorder: Completes worksheets which all will sign off!

Step 3. Set the Lesson.

State the following directions and concepts in language your students understand:

a. Task: Solve each problem correctly; label each diagram, define each term.
b. Positive interdependence: Each student may "share" his or her own geometry notebook (containing definitions and illustrations). One worksheet!
c. Individual accountability: Each should write out any computation. There will be a quiz tomorrow!
d. Criteria for success: Based on school percentages, grade will be given to each individual. Any student without notebook will lose 5% points. Group certificates will be awarded based on performance.
e. Specific behaviors expected: Make sure all students are computing computations.

Step 4. Monitor and Process

a. Evidence of expected behaviors (appropriate actions): Checker and teacher will note names of those not prepared with up-to-date notebooks.

b. Plans for processing: Group will receive worksheets back to evaluate and discuss errors and successes.

Step 5. Evaluate Outcomes

a. Task achievement: Compared results of this cooperative lesson with a class who did it all individually.

b. Group functioning: Those who were not ready did benefit and learned material from those who were.

c. Notes on individuals: Note students who did not come to group prepared to "help" with answers (Notebooks).

d. Suggestions for next time: Use "cooperative" lesson in both math classes.

Perimeter Worksheet

Perimeter—the distance around a polygon

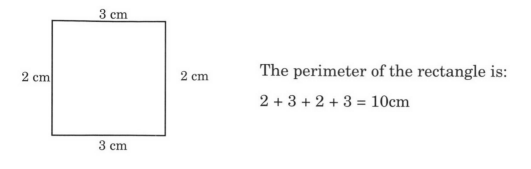

The perimeter of the rectangle is:

2 + 3 + 2 + 3 = 10cm

1. What is the perimeter?

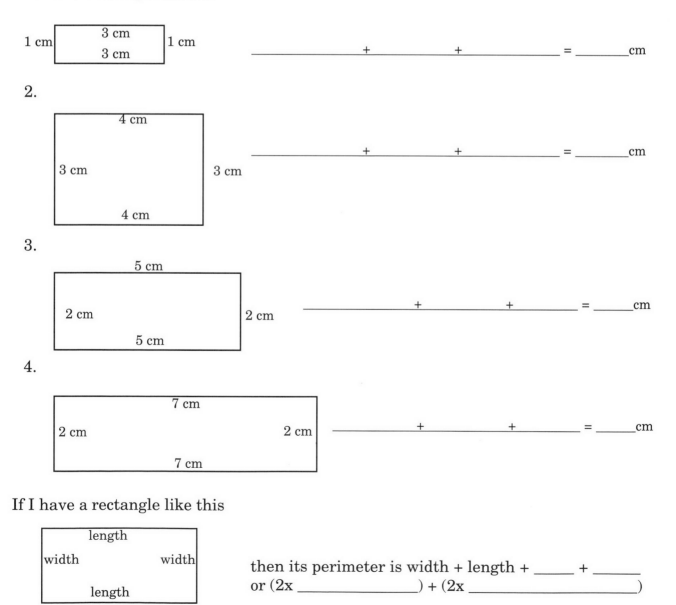

_____ + _____ + _____ = _____cm

2.

_____ + _____ + _____ = _____cm

3.

_____ + _____ + _____ = _____cm

4.

_____ + _____ + _____ = _____cm

If I have a rectangle like this

then its perimeter is width + length + _____ + _____

or (2x _____) + (2x _____)

Triangles

The sum of the measures of the angles in a triangle is *always* 180°

Triangles described by their angles: Triangles described by their sides:

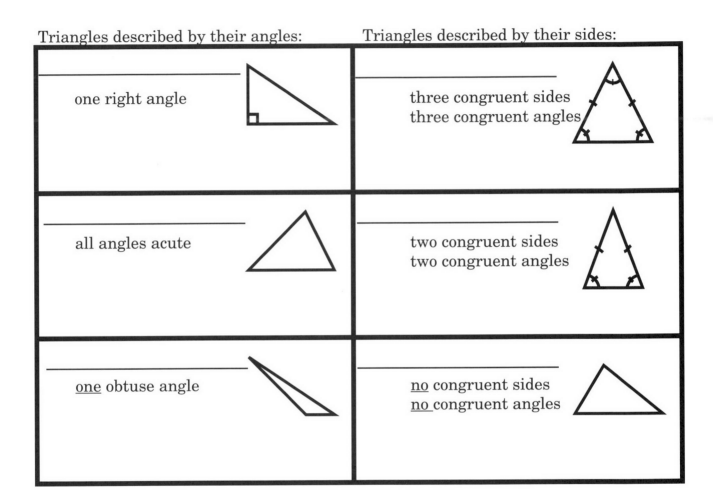

_____	_____
one right angle	three congruent sides three congruent angles
_____	_____
all angles acute	two congruent sides two congruent angles
_____	_____
<u>one</u> obtuse angle	<u>no</u> congruent sides <u>no</u> congruent angles

<u>Combination triangles</u>

This triangle is isosceles and _____.

This triangle is acute and _____.

This triangle is _____ and obtuse.

This triangle is _____, _____,
and isosceles.

Polygons

DEFINITIONS:

A polygon is _____

_____

Congruent means _____

A regular polygon is _____

PICTURES:

POLYGON	# OF SIDES
Triangle	
Quadrilateral	
Pentagon	
Hexagon	
Octagon	

MATH MIXED NUMBER WORKSHEET
by
Joe Stedman

Grade: Sixth

Subject Area: Mathematics

I. Decisions

Lessons: Cooperate to complete math worksheet and insure that all students understand mixed numbers.

Group Size: Three

Group Assignments: Heterogeneous groups assigned by teacher.

Materials: One pencil and one worksheet per group. One crayon, also.

II. Set the Lesson

Academic Task: Complete worksheet on mixed numbers.

Criteria for Success: Complete worksheet with 80% correct.

Positive Interdependence:
One set of materials per group. Assigned roles: Recorder, Encourager, Materials Supplier.

Individual Accountability:
When worksheet is graded, any person in the group may be required to discuss results.

Expected Behaviors: Voluntary participation, speech, eye contact, face-to-face interaction.

III. Monitoring

Monitoring: Will be done by the teacher.

Focus will be on: Individual groups and individual.

Observation sheet includes the behaviors of:
Speaking voluntarily, eye contact, face-to-face interaction.

Processing/Feedback: Will take place at end of period when worksheet is graded (each group grades their own). Most feedback will come from the children and will concentrate on positive outcomes.

All Mixed Up

Pick a fraction from the Fraction Box.
Color the shapes to show that fraction.

Write the fraction on the line next to the shapes.

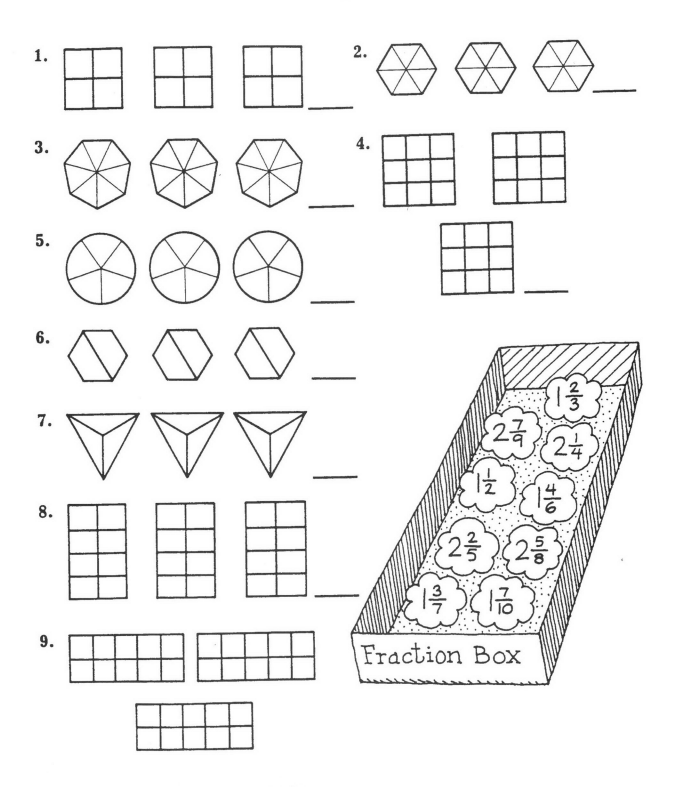

MATH OLYMPICS

by
Karen Shafer

Grade(s):   7-9

Content: Mathematics/Adaptable to any subject

Group Size: Teams of three.   **Assigned Roles:**   Sprinter-runner
Record keeper-recorder
Reporter-read and report

Background: To most middle grade students, the teacher directive to "Study for tomorrow's math test" is met with confusion and frustration. "You can't study math" is the common reply. And, if the test is a chapter, unit or semester exam, students are overwhelmed by the enormity of the task. To assist students in the review process and to help build problem solving skills in a cooperative environment, the Math Olympics were born. Although developed as a math lesson, the Olympics could be adapted to a review in any subject.

Materials: Teacher prepared task cards:one problem or question per card, or commercially prepared task cards for problem solving practice within topical area (integers, fractions, geometry, etc.)
Pencil and paper
Overhead transparency for answers

Set: When used as a test review, help students focus by either asking them to tell you what topics were covered in the chapter (unit, grading period, semester, etc.) that will be covered on the test or by presenting that information to them. "On Friday we are having a test on measurement in geometry. Let's remember what we covered in this chapter..."

Objective: Students will review and practice problem solving single answer math problems and will practice problem solving skills.

Task: The teacher prepares the "events", the task cards, writing one question or problem per card. The game may be structured so that all problems or questions are worth the same number of points, or so that points are awarded according to difficulty. Instructions for the variation follow the basic set of instructions. On the back, number each task card from first to last. Before the games begin, spread the cards on a table in the front of the room so that they are in order. Instruct the Record Keeper to number the team answer sheet from one to the last number and to write all team names on the paper. The rules for competing are that 1) only the Sprinters may be out of their seats to get a card, 2) events may be completed in any order but the answers must be written next to the number that matches the number on the card, 3) each group may be in possession of only one card at a time and 4) all answers must be legible. At the given signal, the Sprinter from each group goes to the card table, gets any card carries it back to the team and hands it to the Reporter. The Reporter reads/interprets the question and the team attempts to answer it. The Record Keeper records the team's answer in the appropriate space. The Sprinter returns the answered card to the table and gets another one. This process continues until time is called. Collect all cards and instruct the Reporter to check that all answers on the team answer sheet are legible. Have teams trade answer sheets. Put the answers on the overhead and have the other team check them. One point is awarded for each correct answer and the total number of points is written and circled at the top of the page. The papers are returned to the original team and are double-checked. The teacher mediates any challenges.

Medals (or certificates) are awarded as follows:

GOLD to all teams with 95% or more of the answers correct

SILVER to all teams with 85% or more of the answers correct

BRONZE to all teams with 75% or more of the answers correct

SPECIAL AWARDS are also given to the top scoring team and to the most improved team.

VARIATION FOR POINTS AWARDED ACCORDING TO DIFFICULTY

When the event/task cards are numbered, color code the numbers according to level of difficulty (EASY-red, MODERATE-green, DIFFICULT-blue). Spread the cards on the table by difficulty category. The Record Keeper folds the team's answer sheet into 3 columns, labeling each at the top with the category, numbering, according to your instructions, the number of problems in each category (EASY #1-9, MODERATE #10-22, DIFFICULT #23-30.) Teams may choose to compete in any event, in any category, in any order. Play commences as above. To score, award one point for each correct EASY answer, two points for each correct MODERATE answer and three points for each DIFFICULT answer.

Processing: Allow time for teams to rework problems that were incorrect - possibly by combining groups, allowing one group to explain missed answers to another or by asking representatives from groups to work problems in front of the class (helping to insure individual accountability.)

Assignment: The actual Olympic games will probably take one class period. The first time the technique is used, it is a good idea to limit the number of task cards to 15-20 to allow adequate explanation, processing and closure time. The processing may take place on a second day to allow adequate time for correcting missed questions.

Closure: As a final emphasis, review precisely what topics and kinds of questions will be on the test, relating them to the kinds of questions on the task cards. Assist students in understanding HOW they can study for a math test by helping them to utilize the resources in their textbooks: assigning or recommending specific test review exercises, pointing out the pages that review vocabulary and concepts and guiding them to the text's written explanations and examples in glossaries and appendices.

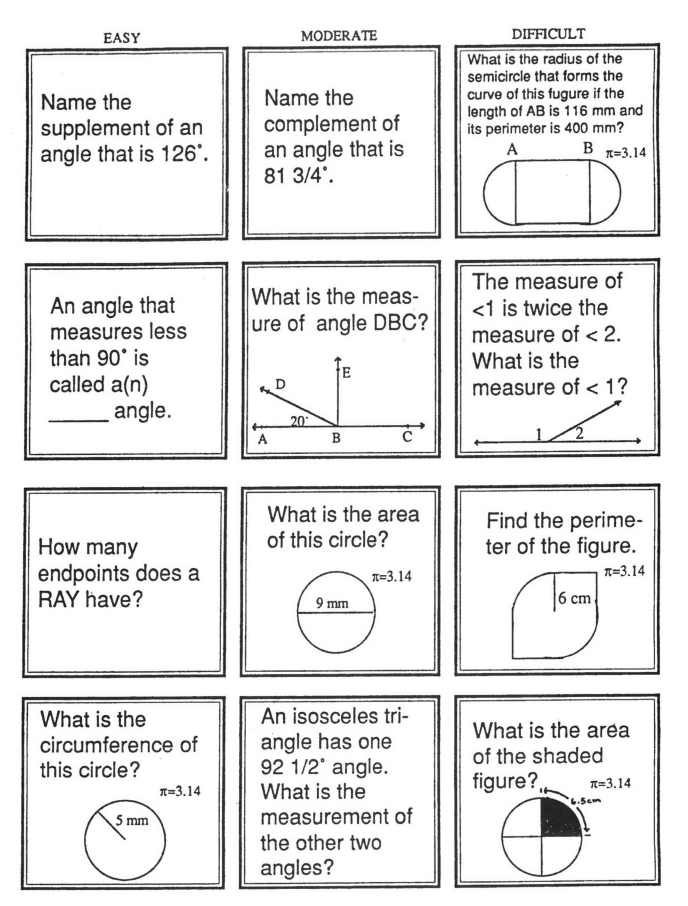

EASY

Name the supplement of an angle that is 126°.

An angle that measures less than 90° is called a(n) _____ angle.

How many endpoints does a RAY have?

What is the circumference of this circle?
π=3.14
5 mm

MODERATE

Name the complement of an angle that is 81 3/4°.

What is the measure of angle DBC?
D
E
20°
A   B   C

What is the area of this circle?
π=3.14
9 mm

An isosceles triangle has one 92 1/2° angle. What is the measurement of the other two angles?

DIFFICULT

What is the radius of the semicircle that forms the curve of this fugure if the length of AB is 116 mm and its perimeter is 400 mm?
A   B   π=3.14

The measure of <1 is twice the measure of < 2. What is the measure of < 1?
1   2

Find the perimeter of the figure.
π=3.14
6 cm

What is the area of the shaded figure?
π=3.14
6.5cm

MATH PROBLEM SOLVING
by
Mary Wingate

Group Size: Three students per group assigned by teacher.

Assignment to Groups: Each group must solve the two problems on the accompanying handout by working together. Students must explain the strategy used to find the answer.

Materials: Each group is given one paper with the problems written on it. They may each have their own pencil.

Academic Task: Solve the problem by using one of the strategies discussed in class. The solution must be shown on the handout and all members of the group must be able to explain the solution.

Criteria for Success: One of the two problems must be answered successfully to earn credit for the task. The explanation of the solution as well as the answer must be written down.

Positive Interdependence: The group turns in one completed paper and they all receive the same grade.

Individual Accountability: Each student from the group must be able to explain the solution their group found. Students will be called on randomly to explain their answer and if they cannot, the group suffers. They all must be able to answer one problem. Another way to check individual work is to have the same problem(s) on a quiz.

Expected Behaviors: Students must work quietly in their group—without raising their voices. They must also involve all members and listen to each member's ideas. One student will act as reader and one as the recorder for the group.

Monitoring: To be done by teacher.

Focus: Will be on individual groups.

Processing: Discussion will be held as to correct ways of solving the problems and following that the pros and cons of the day will be mentioned. To end the lesson, the teacher will summarize the class period in the areas of behavior as a group, math content and overall positives that can be mentioned.

Video Villa is giving away free tokens to anyone who can solve this puzzle:

Place the numbers 1-9 in the squares so that none of the rows, columns, or diagonals have the same sum.

Amy won a free token. What was her solution? (Hint: make a guess; then check your answer.)

Tubby Twophat was determined to win the pie-eating contest at the county fair. He went into training for 6 days. Each day he ate 4 more pies than the day before. Tubby ate 150 pies while in training. How many pies did he eat each day? (Hint: make a guess; then check your guess.)

MEASUREMENT IN MATH

by
Guy Calabrese

Grade:	6 - 8
Group Size:	Three
Assigned Roles:	Scribe—records information; Orator—public speaker/reporter (helps measurer); Measurer—measures different areas (rooms, halls, etc.)
Background:	Math students traditionally think that math courses do not apply to real life situations. This lesson should prove to students that math is applicable to everyday life.
Materials:	Pencil, paper, clipboard, tape measure
Set:	The students are employees of Reedy Paint & Carpet Company. They are estimators. They are to measure various walls, rooms, & hallways in the schol to determine perimeters and areas. They need the perimeter measurement to determine the cost of wood trim. They need the area measurements of the floors for the carpet. They need the area measurements of the wall for the paint cost. They are given two different costs of different materials so that the students have two different estimates for the completed job.
Objective:	The students will compute all measurements into areas and perimeters. They then, in turn, will compute these measurements into cost of materials and labor. They will use their implicit thinking skills for projecting and summarizing.
Task:	See set objectives.
Processing:	Since the groups will be working independently from the class, an observer will be assigned to monitor groups' work. Social skills will be recorded. Working independently, cooperation, 6" voices, and sharing will be observed.
Assignment:	This assignment could very well take two or three days to complete. I would suggest letting one group at a time out of the classroom to measure various rooms, hallways, and halls (pre-determined).
Closure:	Each group will share with the class their estimates to complete the job. They will, in turn, discuss the cost of building maintenance and upkeep and hopefully realize the high cost of building maintenance and the importance of mathematics (perimeters, areas, estimation, addition, subtraction, multiplication, division) in day to day living.

NUMBER GAMES

by
Mary Ellen Holzinger

I.   Lesson: Number Games

II.   Decisions:

Group Size:	Three students per group
Group Assignments:	Count off by threes
Room Arrangement:	Three chairs around a single desk.

Materials needed for each group:

One worksheet per student but only the recorder will write on his/her worksheet.

Assigning roles: On slips of paper have children in each group select roles of recorder, checker, and encourager.

III. Set the Lesson:

Task: Complete the worksheet with only the recorder writing the answers on his/her sheet and only after they all agree.

Positive interdependence:

Each student must contribute his/her part. The recorder may only write down answers that all agree upon. The checker and encourager are as important within the group as the recorder. They will pass or fail together.

Individual accountability:

Each student is responsible for explaining any of the arrived answers. If given a similar exercise, each child should under stand the task easily.

Criteria for success:

Game 1:		Game 2:	
25-27 points = A		Correct = A	
23-24 points = B		Incorrect = D	
20-22 points = C			
Below 20 points = D			

Total grade: Average of Game 1 and Game 2

Behaviors expected: Groups are to work quietly and quickly. (Time limit 20-25 minutes maximum). Insist on Checker and Encourager doing their role.

IV.   Monitor and Process: Evidence of expected behavior: Quiet discussion and contributions, taking turns, leaning in, doodling on scrap paper, serious thinking, especially with Game 2.

Observation: Plans for processing: Teacher will circulate around groups providing positive encouragement and reinforcement. Remind students of roles. Correct group work as they complete if within the time limit. Award stickers for quiet groups who successfully finished the task early. Also, provide another fun enrichment activity for groups finished ahead of time (Numbers within shapes).

PHONE NUMBER DIVISION
by
Cindy Mohen

Grade: 6

Content: Long division and averaging

Group Size: Four

Assigned Roles: Calculator, Chairman, Leader

Background: The students complete this activity after finishing division with two and three digit divisors.

Materials: Paper, pencils

Set: Each student is asked to write down his telephone number, including the area code and excluding the hyphen. The area code will be the divisor; the phone number becomes the dividend. (Any student with no phone can use the school phone number.)

Objective: The students will practice long division and averaging; basic and facts.

Task: The "leader" is the person whose phone number totals the highest sum. Each group member is asked to complete his "phone number division" problem (5 min.). Then each passes his problem to the person on his right. Next, each checks the division problem. The person with the highest quotient becomes the "calculator." He calculates the average quotient for the group. The "leader" then staples all papers together and has group members sign the averaging sheet.

Processing: Each person in the group is asked to take down at least one phone number from a member of the group to use in the future if he needs to call someone with a question concerning math homework.

Assignment: (Homework) Divide the phone number taken down from a group member. If all members of the group do the division problems correctly, each receives, a "free homework pass."

Closure: The "chairman" puts the chairs back in order at the end of the group activity.

PROBLEM SOLVING IN MATH
by
Pam White

Grade Level: 6th

Step 1. Make Decisions:
    a. Group Size: Three
    b. Assignment to groups: Teacher
    c. Room arrangement: Table (hexagon)
    d. Materials needed for each group:
               Problem Solving Worksheet
    e. Assigning Roles: Reader - reads problem aloud to the group. Recorder - writes problem and answers.

Step 2. Set the Lesson:
    a. Task: The reader is to read the problem. You are to discuss the problem and come to a consensus on how to solve the problem. Each of you will work the problem and then come up with one answer. The recorder will write the problem and answer on the group worksheet. I will call on one of you to explain how you solved the problem. Be sure you know how to work each problem.
    b. Positive Interdependence:
               One sheet - one answer accepted.
    c. Individual accountability:
               Each must know how to solve problem and be able to explain to the teacher.
    d. Criteria for success: If 80% of problems are completed correctly.
    e. Specific behaviors expected:
               I expect to see: 1) All students able to phrase question. 2) Know what operation is expected and be able to solve problem. 3) Listen to possible solutions.

Step 3. Monitor and Process
    a. Evidence of expected behaviors.
               All students take part. All are able to solve problems.
    b. Observation form: None
        Observer: Teacher
    c. Plans for processing (feedback):
               Comment on everyone contributing, on agreement of answers, encouraging others.

Step 4. Evaluate Outcomes
    a. Task achievement: Worksheet answers and ability to answer questions.
    b. Group functioning: Did they work together?
    c. Notes on individuals: Note those with trouble.
    d. Suggestions for next time:
               Go over terms that signal operations.

TANGRAMS

by
Mary K. Vanden Avond

Content:	Mathematics
Grade:	6-8
Group Size:	Two members per group (three if necessary).
Assigned Roles:	Give each student a shape and those students with the same shapes will be a group. The teacher will be the observer.
Lesson Title:	Tangram - Cooperative Learning
Background:	No special room arrangement, just so all are able to see the overhead.
Materials:	Each group will work with one set of tangrams.
Set:	Use quiet voices, take turns frequently, and praise.
Objective:	Every member of the group will be able to solve the tangram.
Task:	To use all seven pieces to make the picture shown on the overhead screen.
Assignment:	Every member of the group will be able to solve the tangram. The teacher will randomly call on one member of the group to explain how they solved the tangram. All members must work together on one strategy until they feel that strategy will not work. Then another member's strategy will be tried. This will continue until the tangram is solved. If after 10 minutes, the tangram is still unsolved, clues to solving it will be given.
	Each group will be given one set of tangrams. The task is to use all seven pieces to make the picture shown on the overhead screen. The group's completed tangram must be exactly like the one on the screen - no variations.
Processing:	The class will be asked:
	1. To name several ways on how their group worked well together.
	2. One thing that the group could do better next time they work together.
Closure:	Each group member needs to share their problem solving strategies that they feel will solve the tangram.

Tangrams

Triangles 2 and 8 and triangles 4 and 5 are interchangeable. Possible solutions include:

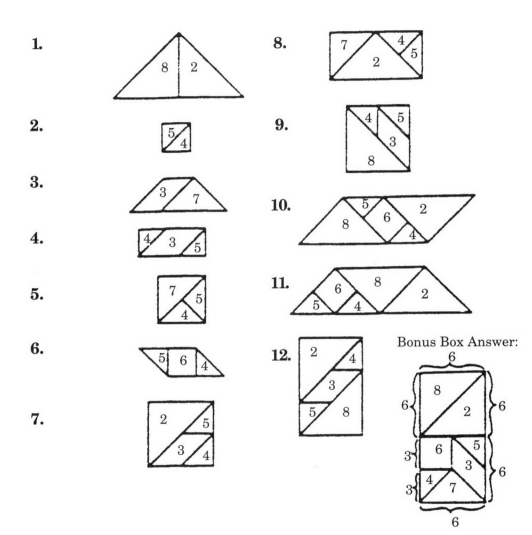

1.

2.

3.

4.

5.

6.

7.

8.

9.

10.

11.

12.

Bonus Box Answer:

P = 36 units

USING WORKSHEETS IN MATH
by
Sue Jessee

Grade Level: 5

Subject Area: Math

Step 1. **Select a Lesson:** Problem Solving - Use or make a table. Lessons 5 (p. 78) and 6 (p. 79) from "The Problem Solver" by Creative Publications

Step 2. **Make Decisions.**
a. Group size: 3-4 students
b. Assignment to groups: Previous groupings. Those groups with only three students will not utilize a student observer.
c. Room Arrangement: Students will gather around the room on the floor in their groups.
d. Materials needed for each group: Pencil. One worksheet #5 per group. One observation sheet per group. Role cards.
e. Assigning roles: Pass out role cards - Reader, encourager, checker, observer.

Step 3. **Set the Lesson.**
a. Task: Successfully complete worksheet #5 as a group and worksheet #6 independently.
b. Positive interdependence: One worksheet #5 per group. If all children in group successfully complete worksheet #6 independently, everyone in group will get double stickers.
c. Individual accountability: Each student will individually be able to explain how the solution is achieved. All members will sign sheet #5.
d. Criteria for success: Students will complete worksheet #6 independently, arriving at the correct solution.
e. Specific behaviors expected: Children will be performing their roles, discussing problem, and cooperating. Emphasis on the role of checker.

See:	heads together	Hear:	6-inch voices
	eye contact		Do you agree?
	bodies facing		Do you understand?

Step 4. **Monitor and Process**
a. Evidence of expected behaviors (appropriate actions): See "heads together," students discussing. Checkers will be checking for understanding and agreement
b. Observation form: Observation sheet
Observer(s): Student - except for groups with only 3, teacher will observe.
c. Plans for processing (feedback): Discuss group successes and problems. Discuss what to work on next time.

Step 5. **Evaluate Outcomes**
a. Task achievement: Problem solving worksheet #5 was completed easily. Compliment the noise level.
b. Group functioning: Most groups worked together efficiently. Noise level was low.
c. Notes on individuals: Jake was not participating.
d. Suggestions for next time: People not participating should concentrate on improving participation. Encourager should help draw them in. The next lesson will focus on the role of the encourager.

Use or Make a Table

Marvin Monkey wanted to start a school. So he counted all the young monkeys in his jungle. When Marvin finished counting, he gave these clues:

- There were more than 25
- There were fewer than 40
- I said the number when I counted by fives.
- I didn't say the number when I counted by tens.

How many young monkeys did Marvin count?

FIND OUT
- What is the question you have to answer?
- What did Marvin do?
- What do Marvin's clues tell you about the number of young monkeys in his jungle?

CHOOSE A STRATEGY
- Circle to show what you choose.

SOLVE IT
- What is the highest number in Marvin's clues? Use that as the highest number in the table started below. What is the lowest number in Marvin's clues? Use that as the lowest number in the table. Fill in the numbers between 25 and 40.
- What does the first clue tell you? Could 25 be the number Marvin counted? If not, cross it out. Could each of the other numbers in the table be the number?
- What does the second clue tell you? Could 40 be the number Marvin counted? If not, cross it out. Could each of the other numbers in the table be the number?
- What does the third clue tell you? Which of the numbers left in the table could be Marvin's number? Cross out all the other numbers.
- What does the fourth clue tell you? Then which of the two numbers tells how many young monkeys Marvin counted?

25		40

LOOK BACK
- Look back to see if your answer fits with what the problem tells you and asks you to find. Read the problem again. Look back over your work. Does your answer fit?

Use or Make a Table

Ariel rides the Starlight Express from Misty Station to her home. The Starlight Express zooms past 100 stars an hour. Ariel will not tell us how far her home is from Misty Station, but she did give us these clues:

I ride past more than 39 stars.
I ride past fewer than 48 stars.
I ride past an odd number of stars.
One part of the number tells how many letters there are in my name.

How many stars does Ariel pass on her way home?

FIND OUT
- What is the question you have to answer?
- How does Ariel get from Misty Station to her home?
- What do Ariel's clues tell you about the number of stars she passes on her way from Misty Station to her home?
- To answer the main question, do you need to know that the Starlight Express zooms past 100 stars an hour?

CHOOSE A STRATEGY
- Circle to show what you choose.

SOLVE IT
- What is the highest number in Ariel's clues? Use that as the highest number in the table started below. What is the lowest number in Ariel's clues? Use that as the lowest number in the table. Fill in the numbers between the two numbers.
- What does the first clue tell you? Could 39 be the number of stars? Could each of the other numbers be the number?
- What does the second clue tell you? Could 48 be the number of stars? Could each of the other numbers be the number?
- What does the third clue tell you? Which of the remaining numbers could be the number?
- What does the fourth clue tell you? Which of the numbers tells how many stars Ariel passes?

---
39   48

LOOK BACK
- Look back to see if your answer fits with what the problem tells you and asks you to find. Read the problem again. Look back over your work. Does your answer fit?

1987 Creative Publications

WRITING THE EQUATION OF A LINE

by
Anita Vitous

I. Decisions

Lesson: Writing the Equation of a Line

Group Size: Three to a group.

Group Assignments:
    I will assign based on ability.

Materials: Worksheet

II. Set the Lesson

Academic Task:
    Complete the worksheet.

Criteria for Success:

    School grading scale:
       93%-100 = A
       85%- 92 = B
       77%- 84 = C
       70%- 76 = D

Positive Interdependence:
    If all group members achieve above 80% on the test, they will each earn five bonus points.

Individual Accountability:
    Individual tests.

Expected Behaviors:
    Everyone contributes, helps, and listens. Try to encourage each member to be involved. Use quiet voices.

III. Monitoring

Monitoring will be done by:
    The teacher.

Focus will be on:
    Individuals.

Observation sheet includes the behaviors of:
    1) Quiet voices, 2) Praising, 3) Taking turns.

Processing/Feedback:
    1) Have each group list three things they did well, and one thing they will try to do better.
    2) Using the teacher's observation sheet, discuss observations.

Graphing Activity

Find the equations of the lines graphed in the accompanying graphs. Each small square measures 1 unit on a side.

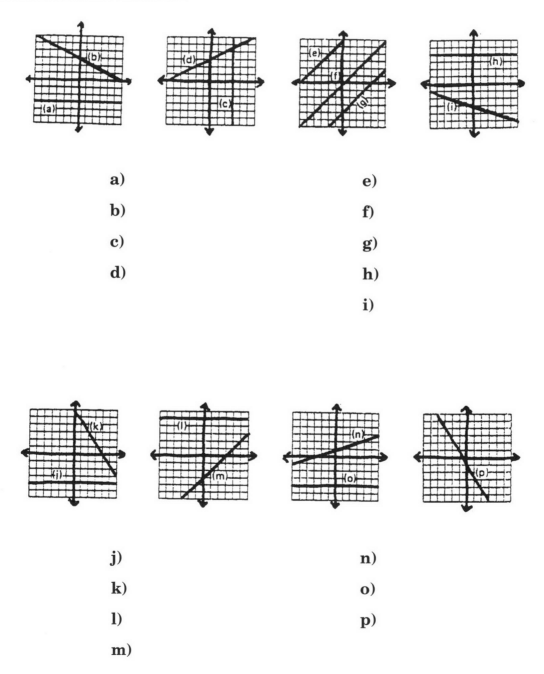

a)

b)

c)

d)

e)

f)

g)

h)

i)

j)

k)

l)

m)

n)

o)

p)

Music

In pursuit of some group activities, students utilize materials beyond the classroom.

CONTEMPORARY MUSIC SOUNDS
by
Beth Allen

6th Grade Music

I.   Select a Lesson

Lesson: Creating a piece of contemporary music using body sounds.

II.   Make Decisions

Group size: 5

Assignment will be done according to ability levels; each group will have "high" and "low" students.

Room: Students will pull their chairs into circles for each group; groups will be widely dispersed throughout the room.

Materials needed: One music text for each student; a watch with a second hand/digital counter.

Roles: Timekeeper, each sound.

III.   Set the Lesson

You will work together to perform the piece according to the directions and symbols in your book. Your performance grade depends on each person doing his or her job properly.

I will also give each person a grade based on my observations of your work during practice time. I will be listening for correct dynamic levels and rhythms in your performance.

IV.   Monitor and Process

I expect to see heads together, and eye contact while you practice; I will be listening for each part performed when your timekeeper indicates.

I should see groups clumped together, looking at their musical scores. I should hear different sounds coming out of each mouth only when it is written in the score.

V.   Evaluate Outcomes

Sheet with each student's name - I will check each time I hear him/her performing job, and make a special note of help given to others. I will be the sole observer.

Discussion of how their performances went; what was easiest, hardest about working in that group; if they had to do it again, how would they do it differently?

The students as a whole performed the piece accurately and well. One group did not stick to the time constraints given in the music.

KEY SIGNATURES - E^b

by
Barbara Kaminsky

Grade: 6 & 7

Content: Beginning Band

Group Size: Five teams of eight

Assigned Roles: Leader
Listener

Background: Beginning band classes often number between 35 to 50 students per class. The typical band class has varied levels of ability—low, middle, and high academic achievers. Much attention is focused on tone production, correct fingering of notes, and proper posture. By using small groups within the large band class, more attention can be given to each child. Thus, the material used in class is covered more thoroughly and a higher percentage of comprehension is achieved.

Materials: Method book, pencil, staff paper.

Set: To set the stage for the small groups, review the key signature of Concert E*b* with the entire class. Have each section of the band (e.g. clarinet, flute, etc) play the scale and arpeggio. Make sure that all new fingerings are covered.

Objective: The students will practice several pages of music in their method book using the Concert E*b* key signature. Recognition of this key signature will become auto matic - the students will be able to realize the different fingerings used for this key signature.

Task: Explain to the students that they will be working on recognizing the Concert E*b* key signature on several pages in their method book.

Each group will consist of eight students comprised of different instruments—not *like* instruments.

Each group will have a music symbol for its group name—whole note, half note, quarter note, eighth note, dotted half note. Assign each student a music symbol.

Draw a chart on the blackboard of the location of each group using the music symbols.

Next, instruct the students that each is responsible for his/her own stand, chair, book, pencil, and instrument. Inform the students that they will be given two minutes to get to their location. No talking is permitted. At the end of two minutes a signal (THREE LOUD CLAPS) will be given. At that time they should be in place. A grade is given to each group for their group effort of getting to the correct location with all of the required materials. (I repeat this procedure until the students do this in the given time frame.)

Once the groups are in location, assign each group a LEADER and a LISTENER. The job of the LEADER is to set the tempo for the group (the leader plays along with the group). The job of the LISTENER is to make sure everyone is counting correctly and playing the correct pitches (the LISTENER does not play along with the group until everyone is secure with their notes and rhythms). Assign each group a specific line of music.

The time frame for each group to work on a line of music is six minutes. After the six minutes is up, signal the groups (THREE CLAPS) to stop playing.

Processing: Have each group play their line of music. Assign each group a grade based on their playing. Remind the class that all groups will have the opportunity to play the same line of music during the week. This keeps each student focusing his/her attention on what the other groups are playing as well as his/her own group.

Assignment: This lesson will take three or four days. At the end of each day, remind the class that attention is being focused on the key signature.

Closure: As a class, review all lines of music with the Concert E♭ key signature.

Next, use a concert piece of music which has the Concert E♭ key signature.

Reading/Language Arts

**Social skills learned will be important
to students the rest of their lives.**

COMPREHENSION/REVIEW
OF SELECTED READING MATERIAL

by
Guadalupe Jimenez

Grade Level: 6-8

Subject Area: Reading

Step 1. **Select a Lesson:** Answer comprehension questions of a given reading selection to review for comprehension test of that given selection.

Step 2. **Make Decisions.**
   a. Group size: 3 students in each of 4 groups
   b. Assignment to groups: Each group will be assigned 2 comprehension questions to discuss an answer. Then all groups will share answers.
   c. Room arrangement: Student desks are joined together in groups of 4.
   d. Materials needed for each group: Basal reader and comprehensionworksheet
   e. Assigning roles: 1 reader, 1 recorder, 1 runner and 1 observer.

Step 3. **Set the Lesson.**
   a. Task: Be able to jigsaw review questions in preparation for a comprehension test.
   b. Positive interdependence: Share resource, environment (desks joined together); Each member has a role. Each has a common goal.
   c. Individual accountability: Each member is responsible to know answers and be able to justify them.
   d. Criteria for success: After answers are shared, each student must be able to answer all the questions assigned correctly.
   e. Specific behaviors expected: All students must be actively engaged, agree on answers, take turns, listen carefully, be encouraging and supportive.

Step 4. **Monitor and Process**
   a. Evidence of expected behaviors (appropriate actions): Students will have direct eye contact, will be attentive, each will assume the roles.
   b. Observation form: Sheet will record positive behaviors.
   c. Plans for processing (feedback): Take time to regroup and share information. Point out positive behaviors.

Step 5. **Evaluate Outcomes**
   a. Task achievement: Each group member will be able to answer questions correctly and be able to justify them.
   b. Group functioning: All executed their roles and agreed on answers.
   c. Notes on individuals: Teacher circulated around the room and monitored group progress.
   d. Suggestions: Teacher can write down questions and answers given on the board to model for the students the correct way of answering complete and meaningful answers.

DESCRIPTIVE PARAGRAPH WRITING
by
Ann Mitchell

Grade Level: 6

Subject Area: Language Arts

I.   Decisions:

After having been previously introduced to describng words, students will write
a descriptive paragraph using describing words to tell about their animal picture.
Later, groups will share their description and the class will guess what the
animal is.

Group Size:	3 individuals per group
Group Assignments:	Hand out individual cards with animal character names on them. Matching cards will be in the same group.
Materials:	Each group will receive a picture of an animal, one pencil and writing paper.

II.   Set the Lesson

Academic Task:	After the teacher reads *Aminal* by Lorra Balian, and modeling a description, students will work in groups of three to write a description of an animal. Use describing words to tell about their animal picture. After having written their description, the teacher will randomly call on a member of each group to share the description. Class will guess what it describes.
Criteria for Success:	100% if the class can guess what the animal is. 90% if group has described at least four different parts of the animal 80% -3 different parts 70% - 2 different parts.
Positive Interdependence:	

Each member of the group will have a job which is necessary for the group to be successful:
1. Encourager
2. Checker
3. Recorder

Individual Accountability:

Each member will be able to read/tell their description to
the class.

Expected Behaviors:	Students should be facing each other, and talking with a 12 inch voice. Each student should contribute and help other groupmembers to contribute for completion. Students should listen to each other.

III. Monitoring

Will be done by: Teacher

Focus will be on: Whole class, individual groups and individuals

Observation sheet includes the behaviors of:
Using a twelve inch voice, checing to make sure each member is involved.

Processing/Feedback: The instructor will move around the room providing positive reinforcement to both individuals and groups for their success at completing the academic task and the social skills. After the completed lesson each group will discuss how well they did (both socially and academically). Also, discuss future goals.

IDENTIFYING MAIN IDEA

by
Shirley Posey

Grade Level: 6

Subject Area: Reading

Time: 20 minutes

Step 1:   **Select a Lesson:** Group members work cooperatively to identify the main idea and at least 4 supporting detail sentences of each of two Weekly Reader articles.

Step 2:   **Make Decisions:**

a. Group size: 3

b. Assignment to groups: Because we have 22 students in our class, we will count off by 7s. The ONES will belong to one group, the TWOS to another, and so on. In the event there is an odd student, there will be one group of 4.

c. Room arrangement: Face-to-face with a table in between.

d. Materials needed for each group: 1 issue of *Weekly Reader,* 1 pencil, and 1 recording worksheet. Also, 1 set of role cards.

e. Assigning roles: Reader, paraphraser, and recorded/checker. Count off 1, 2, and 3 within each group: Ones are Readers. Twos are paraphrasers. Threes are Recorders/Checkers. In the possible event of one group of 4, students will count off 1, 2, 3, and 4. Ones' and Twos' roles will remain the same as above, Three will be the Recorder, and Four will be the checker.

Step 3:   **Set the Lesson**

a. Task: Each group will be given one *Weekly Reader* and one recording worksheet on which to identify, in writing, the main idea and at least 4 supporting detail sentences for each of 2 selected articles.

b. Positive Interdependence: To foster positive interdependence, each group will have a single *Weekly Reader* and a single recording worksheet. Students will be assigned roles. There will be a group reward of "$100" for each member to spend at our classroom "store" if each correctly identifies the main idea and 4 supporting detail sentences of 2 different Weekly Reader articles.

c. Individual Accountability: Using 2 different *Weekly Reader* articles, students will be tested individually on their ability to correctly identify the main idea and at least 4 supporting detail sentences for each of the articles. Also, the instructor will randomly select students to identify main idea and/or supporting detail sentences orally, on the chalkboard, or on an overhead.

d. Criteria for Success: 100% (A) Fantastic, 90% (B) Very Good, 80% (c) Good

e. Specific Behaviors Expected: Quiet voices, the contributing of ideas, checking to make sure that everyone in the group agrees with the answers before same are recorded, accurately listening to reader, and the criticizing of ideas, not people.

Step 4: **Monitor and Process**

Instructor will monitor group for active listening, checking, using diplomacy, using quiet voices, and contributing of ideas and giving praise and positive feedback for same.

LITERATURE RESPONSE GROUPS
by
Hanson/Prentice

Purposes:

To help students learn to enjoy reading. To help students acquire insights into how written language works.

Suggestions for Use:

This activity is designed as an alternative to traditional basal reading groups in middle schools. Literature response groups can serve as a major element in a whole language classroom reading program or as a 2-4 week "break" from basal readers. To prepare for literature response groups, the teacher must gather sets of books that will be of interest to the students. Sets can be three copies of the same book, different books by the same author, books on the same topic, or books in the same genre.

Procedure:

1. Place the students in heterogeneous groups of three. Explain that for the next several weeks in reading they will work in these groups and read from the sets of books in the classroom. New sets of books can be added if groups identify authors, topics, titles or genre they would like to read.

2. Have the group identify one person as the chooser, one as the questioner, and one as the recorder. Explain that each person will assume a new role for the next book the group reads.

3. Have the chooser from each group select a set of books for the group.

4. Everyone reads silently for 20-30 minutes. Anyone who finishes reading the book before the silent reading time is up should read from their "back-up" book. The teacher should read during this time also.

5. At the end of the silent reading, the questioners get the question sheets from the teacher. Each group, regardless of what they are reading, gets the same question. The questions should be written on index cards or half-sheets of paper. Sample question: List two characteristics of the main character in your story.

6. The questioner reads the question to the trio. The group talks about the question for a few minutes. Once the group agrees on a response to the question, the recorder writes the response on the sheet and all members sign the sheet indicating that they understand and agree with the response. The teacher should move from group to group eavesdropping to identify themes emerging from the discussion and to get ideas for the question for tomorrow.

7. Then the entire class discusses the question. Highlight how the answer to the question varies from group to group. Discuss instances where the question didn't seem appropriate for a particular group because of the books they were reading.

8. Have the small groups process the activity by discussing how well they worked together on the task and what they might do tomorrow to do even better.

Literature Response Group Sheet

Book Title:

_____

Where does your story take place? When does your story take place? How does the author let you know the setting?

_____

_____

_____

_____

_____

_____

_____

_____

_____

_____

Group Members: _____

_____

_____

NEWSPAPER HEADLINES
by
Theresa Drendel

I. **Decisions:**

Lesson: Headlines

Group Size: Three

Group Assignments:
Assign a student of low, medium and high ability to each group before class. Tell students groups were selected randomly.

Materials: Ten headlines from recent newspapers and 10 strips of paper for each group of three.

II. **Set the Lesson:**

Academic Task:
Students will predict the storyline of each headline and then class discussion will follow. Students will be informed of the actual story after sharing their ideas. Then, students will be asked to prioritize the headlines according to most important to the world and least important to the world.

Criteria for Success:
Students will be successful if the group reaches a consensus about the priorities.

Positive Interdependence:
Materials interdependence

Individual Accountability:
Teacher will evaluate by observation and discussion.

Expected Behaviors:
Students will be expected to contribute ideas to the group and reach consensus on the priorities.

III. **Monitoring and Feedback:**
This will be done by the teacher observing each group. Groups working well together will receive plus tickets.

(NEWSPAPER HEADLINES continued)

Topic: Predictions, Values, Current Events

Theme: Human Environment Interaction

Grade: 7

Time Needed:
2 - 40 minute periods

Objectives: Students will practice developing higher level thinking skills by predicting. Students will develop cooperative skills within the group. Students will express their opinions.

Format: Cooperative Learning Groups and Discussion

Procedures:

1. Divide students into groups of three. Assign them roles of recorder, time-keeper, encourager.

2. Tell students to copy the headlines from the board onto the strips of paper. Put only one of these actual headlines on each strip.

3. Each group needs to decide what the news story was about. Tell students to spend 3 minutes on each headline. The recorder should write a brief summary. Collect these summaries at the end of class.

4. On day 2, return the group summaries for class discussion. Groups should share predictions and their reason for it.

5. After each discussion, ask or tell students the actual news story.

6. Assign groups to rank the headlines in the order of most important to the world to least important to the world. Have groups try for consensus.

7. Ask groups to share their rankings and their reasons for it.

Evaluation:

Determine by observation if all students shared their opinions. Reward groups working well.

Follow-up:

Possible debate on "hot" issues.

PEER EDITING COMPOSITIONS
by
Margaret Boyer

I. Decisions

Group Size:	3-4
Group Assignment:	Chosen by teacher (high, low and two in between).
Materials:	Peer editing check list, compositions, desks close together

II. Set the Lesson

Academic Task: To edit each member of the group's compositions for several kinds of mistakes.

Criteria for Success: Criteria is the same as that on the peer edit check list.

Positive Interdependence:
Bonus points for every member of a group in which each member receives a particular grade on his/her composition.

Individual Accountability:
Individual grades on a composition.

Expected Behaviors: Use quiet voices, state something you like about the composition and state criticisms positively.

III. Monitoring:

Will be done by:	Teacher
Focus will be on:	Individuals

No observation sheets used.

Processing/Feedback: Class was pulled back together and discussed how well they did as a group. Also, at the bottom of the check list are questions about the performance of each individual as a group member.

EDITING SHEET

YES	NO	GRAMMAR, SPELLING, PUNCTUATION
___	___	I have written my name, the date, and title on my paper.
___	___	I began each sentence with a capital letter.
___	___	I put a period, question mark, or exclamation point at the end of each sentence.
___	___	I put a comma when I paused between ideas in a sentence.
___	___	I left a few spaces before starting each paragraph.
___	___	I spelled each word correctly.
___	___	I put conversations inside quotation marks.

REVISING SHEET

YES	NO	STYLE
___	___	I have used very specific words
___	___	I have used different kinds of sentence patterns.
___	___	I have shifted smoothly from one paragraph to the next.
___	___	I have tied up all my ideas at the end.

READING - CAUSE AND EFFECT

by
Barbara Schultz

Grade Level: 6

Subject: Reading

Group Size: Three

Group Assignments:

Read appropriate pages. Identify three examples of cause and effect.
Write these on the paper, labeling cause "C" and Effect "E."

Room Arrangement:

Three desks facing toward each other. Children EE & KK (eye to eye and knee to knee).

Materials: 1 reading book, 1 pen/pencil, 1 piece of penmanship paper.

Assigning roles: Reader - one with the longest fingers. Recorder - one with the shortest fingers.
Reporter - one who's left.

Task: One person (the reader) will read the paragraphs out loud to the group.

Everyone must listen very carefully and try to identify examples of <u>Cause and Effect</u>. You must find three.

The recorder will write down what your group decides are the examples of cause and effect, labeling Cause "C" and effect "E." D

Do not write until you have discussed it and agreed. Justify your answers to each other orally.

Positive Interdependence:

1 set of materials
All must reach consensus
Each person has a role.

Individual Accountability:

Each student should be able to explain their 3 choices to me.
Each student will have to label examples of cause and effect in a story next week.

Criteria for Success:

All of you will have located 3 examples of cause and effect. If you get all 3 correct, you may take a break between 3rd and 4th hour.

Specific Behaviors Expected:

Make sure you all share and convince each other of your choices. Share your ideas!
Explain your point of view.
Listen to others' points of view.
I expect to hear you asking each other if you agree.
I should see heads nodding and shaking.

Monitoring and Processing Evidence:

Everyone should be involved.
Everyone does his own job.
Eye to eye contact.
Hearing "I agree" and "I disagree" and reasons.
"What do you think?"

I'll write down some notes on my observations as I circulate the room.

We'll discuss how everything went when we're done sharing and make sugges tions for next time. We'll highlight the good things and bad things—my opinions (observations) and theirs.

Discuss problems with coming to a consensus.

Students should all be able to find three examples of cause and effect correctly.

ROLE PLAYING A STORY

by
Ophelia Moore & Sarah Nix

Grade: 6-8

Content: Reading/Language Arts

Group Size: Five

Roles: Reader, four individual characters

Instructional Task:

Students grouped randomly in groups of five will dramatize a fairytale as it is read by the reader.

Positive Interdependence:

Students within each group will cooperatively decide the following:

1) Given a choice of two fairy tales they will decide which one they wish to dramatize.

2) They will cooperatively decide which students will take specific character roles within the group.

3) They will cooperatively decide how their story will be dramatized to best convey the meaning of the story to the audience. (Small props will be given to each group which will assist in its dramatization).

Individual Accountability:

Each member is responsible for appropriately portraying the character to convey the storyline to the audience.

Criteria for Success:

Each member of the group whose group satisfactority completes the productionwill be given a bookmark.

Expected Behaviors:

Social Skill and Content Skill: Each member of the group will share his/her ideas and be a part of the group's effort to successfully dramatize its story for the audience.

Monitoring: See sample Observation Sheet (p. 106).

Processing: See attached group processing sheet.

Ending: Bring positive closure to the lessons by commenting on how the group enjoyed preparation of the lesson.

Notables

GROUP PROCESSING

One word my group could use to describe how we worked together is _____

One statement describing what our group enjoyed best about role playing a story.

_____

_____

_____

106

OBSERVATION SHEET

Group Members:					
Behaviors Observed:					
Move into groups quietly					
Working Together:					
Staying with the group					
Keeping hands & feet to self					
Looking at the group's paper					
Sharing Information:					
Using people's names					
Looking at the speaker					
Discussing pros and cons:					
Listening and explaining:					
Using quiet voices:					
Using no "put downs"					
Complimenting good behavior:					
TOTAL TALLY MARKS:					
Finishing on time/asking each other for help/offering to help & support.					
TOTAL BEHAVIOR POINTS:					

VOCABULARY SKITS

by
Lori O'Conner

Subject Area: Reading

Grade Level: 6

Lesson Summary: The group members will work cooperatively to learn a vocabulary word and present the vocabulary word to the class through a skit.

Instructional Objectives: The students will get practice and help in learning a vocabulary word.

Time Required: 30-40 minutes

Decisions: Group Size: Seven groups of three

Assignment to Groups: Since there are 22 students in the class, I would have the students count off by seven. All the ones would make up a group, all the twos would make up another group, etc.

Roles:

Reader: The reader will look up the vocabulary word in the text and read the sentence in which the word appears. The group will predict the meaning of the word. The reader will write down the predicted definition of the word.

Researcher: The researcher will look up the definition in a dictionary. The researcher will read the definition of the word to the group.

Checker: The checker will have each person paraphrase the definition. The checker will write down the agreed upon definition. Also, the checker will make sure every one agrees on the ideas for the skit.

THE LESSON

Task:

In this lesson you are to:
1. Look up and define a vocabulary word.
2. Understand the definition of the word.
3. Develop a skit to teach the word to the class.

Positive Interdependence:

The tasks will be done cooperatively. This means:
1. One student will have a book and read the sentence in which the word appears to the group.
2. One student will have a dictionary and read the definition to the group.
3. Each member should know the definition of the word.
4. Each member should participate in the writing and performing of the skit.

Individual Accountability:

Each student will be responsible for writing and knowing all seven definitions for the words. After the skits have been performed, I will randomly choose students to repeat the definitions of the seven words. The next day I give the class an individual quiz on the words.

Criteria for Success:

I will know the task has been successful if the students receive the following grades on the quiz: 100% Excellent   86% Good

Expected Behaviors:

I expect to see the following behaviors as I observe the groups:
1. Each student is doing his/her job.
2. Each student is contributing ideas to the group.
3. Each student is using a quiet voice.
4. Thee are no put-downs in the group.

(I would use a T-Chart to explain these desired behaviors. See Chapter 4, p. 38.

Monitoring/Processing/Feedback:

1. The monitoring will be done by the instructor.
2. The focus will be on individual and group members.
3. At the end of the lesson, I would refer back to the T-Chart and stress positive behaviors observed in the groups. Then I would ask the groups to write down one thing that worked well in their group and one thing that needed improvement.

WORD BANK POEMS
by
Cynthia A. Werner

Content: Science/Language

Group Size: Four

Roles: Recorder, Material Manager, Turn-Counter,
Checker, Encourager (extra)

Instructional Task:

To integrate English and Science by brainstorming certain parts of speech (adjectives, adverbs, nouns, verbs) particular to a specific endangered species. These word banks are then used to write individual poems from the animal's point of view—poem pattern being Inside/Outside.

Positive Interdependence:

One word bank per group, one marker for brainstorming, jobs ensure each student must depend on others, turn-counter ensures all get a turn.

Individual Accountability:

Each student produces from that word bank an individual Inside/Outside poem* utilizing all four parts of speech from the animal's point of view. *Outside I see (hear, etc.)/Inside I am (or I feel)......

Criteria for Success:

An original poem utilizing the four basic parts of speech from the animal's point of view.

Expected Behaviors:

Using 2-inch voices and using positive encouraging words. (Also expected to remain with group).

Monitoring: Checklist—group points for 2-inch voices and use of encouraging words. Most points gets stickers.

Processing: Turn to the person on your right and complete this statement. "Thanks for helping by _____."

Ending: Group processing—What did we do well? What should we work on? Sharing and discussion of poems.

WRITING POEMS - "I REMEMBER ....."
by
D. Holmes

Grade:	8
Content:	English/Content Writing
Group Size:	Four
Assigned Roles:	Reader, Researcher, Recorder, and Summarizer
Background:	8th grade students will have numerous activities in the future where brainstorming, dictionary skills and recalling the past is essential to their writing assignments.
Materials:	Pencils, paper, dictionary, thesaurus, and knowledge of figurative language (similes, metaphors, personification, alliteration, etc.)
Set:	To set the stage for this writing activity, review figurative language and recall your own personal experiences by using "I remember ...."

I remember springtime and singing with the birds
while daydreaming under a tremendous tree.
I remember summertime, swimming in freezing, fresh
water lakes and cook-outs with friends.
I remember autumn, reading books, listening to
music, and watching the falling leaves.
And I remember winter, the starry snowy evenings,
and snowbanks as tall as a man.

Objective:	The students will practice their brainstorming, dictionary, and writing skills by writing a poem (with figurative language) using the recipe "I remember.............."
Task:	Explain to the students that "I remember ...." is a recipe for writing poetry. They are to plunge into their memories. Go back as far as they can and rescue their earliest "I remembers ...." They are to brainstorm a list of their memories. Once a list is made, the group is to select the favorite "I remembers....." Using their favorite "I remembers ....", they are to organize these thoughts. After organizing these thoughts, students are to write an "I remember ...." poem (using figurative language). The researcher is to use the dictionary or thesaurus to help if necessary. Next, read the poems aloud. Using the "I remember........" recipe, anyone can write a poem.
Processing:	After reading the poems, discuss how you felt during these "I remembers....." Do these "I remembers........ affect the way you feel about certain experiences today?
Assignment:	The lesson should not take more than one class period, but may be used over again in a variety of ways.
Closure:	As the class discusses the "I remembers...." decide which "I remember........" each liked the most and why.
Future Assignments:	"I remember......." may be used after a short story, novel, or seeing a movie.
Reference:	Berbrich 1977. *Writing Creatively.* New York, N.Y. Amsco School Publications.

Science

A peer can often serve as a teacher.

ASTRONOMY PIONEERS
by
Mary Sykora

Lesson: Who are the Pioneers of Astronomy?

Group size: Four students/group

Assignment to groups: According to class seating. Arrangement in pods.

Roles: 1) materials handler
                2) reader
                3) recorder
                4) reporter

Materials: Set of encyclopedias, One answer sheet/group that includes a set of questions to be answered plus a time line.

Academic task: Write a paragraph that answers the following:
                1) Name of astronomer
                2) Years lived
                3) Country lived in
                4) Discovery or contribution

Indicate on a time line when this person's discovery/discoveries was/were made.

Criteria for Success:
    Answer sheet/timeline/paragraph completed
        100% = super
        90% = Good job
        80% = OK

Positive Interdependence:
    1) Role - students assigned roles within group.
    2) Goal - a product.
    3) Environmental - groups seated in pods of four students each.

Individual Accountability:
    1) When called upon, each student can answer all questions about his/her group's astronomer.
    2) Student will answer quiz questions about his/her astronomer on the following day.

Expected Behaviors: 1) Verbal participation. 2) 6" voices. 3) Stay with the group.

Observation sheet includes a list of the three expected behaviors.

Processing: Verbal discussion:
    1) Did we find the information?
    2) Did everyone participate?
    3) Feeling of success?
    4) Easier than working alone?
    5) Suggestions for improvement.

Astronomers: Draw name from list:
            1) Copernicus
            2) Galileo
            3) Sir Isaac Newton
            4) Herschel & Caroline Herschel
            5) Edmond Halley
            6) Ptolemy
            7) Johannes Kepler

ELECTRON CONFIGURATIONS IN SCIENCE

by
Natalie Weiger

Grade Level: Junior High School

Subject Area: Science

Lesson Summary: Group members work cooperatively to draw electron configurations and ensure all group members can correctly explain their diagrams.

Group Size: Three

Group Assignments: Students will receive random index cards marked with either an element's name, symbol, or atomic number. They then have to find their group-mates by successfully matching a set of three corresponding cards.

Room Arrangement: Students will arrange their stools in groups of three around lab tables.

Materials Needed:

One piece of unlined paper, one pencil, one copy of the Periodic Chart of Elements, one set of directions for each group.

Assigning Roles: Reader/Recorder: Reads the directions aloud to the group and draws configurations

Checker: Checks to make sure all group members understand how to arrive at the answer to each problem and that all agree with each configuration before moving ahead.

Encourager: Invites all members to contribute and keeps the group moving towards their goal

THE LESSON

Task: In this lesson you are to:

1. Complete each of the electron configurations correctly.
2. Understand the way you arrived at your answer.
3. Be able to demonstrate the steps you took to develop your electron configuration.

Positive Independence:

This lesson will be done in cooperative groups, therefore, you must:
1. Produce one set of diagrams that is signed by all group members. (learning goal/resource interdependence)
2. Act in the role assigned to you. (role interdependence)
3. Each achieve 90% or better on a follow-up quiz in order for your group to get a "Mr. Wizard" award (5 extra credit points). (positive reward interdependence)

Individual Accountability:

Each member should be able to defend and explain their diagrams as they will be called on randomly after the task. Also, at the end of the period, each student will take a quiz requiring them to generate an electron configuration on their own.

Criteria for Success:

Percentage points/letter grades used on quiz. Also, if all groups members receive a 90% or higher on the quiz, they each will receive 5 bonus points.

Expected Behaviors:

As this lesson takes place, I should be able to observe:
1. All members performing their assigned roles.
2. Members asking questions when they don't understand.
3. Encouragement dealing with participation and ideas.

MONITOR AND PROCESS

Monitoring: Teacher will monitor the groups to determine any problems with the assignment and to ensure the groups are indeed working collaboratively. Teacher will intervene to correct any misunderstandings of task, misuse or absence of appropriate interpersonal skills, or to reinforce correct use of those skills.

Intervening: Teacher will intervene to correct any misunderstandings of task, misuse or absence of appropriate interpersonal skills, or to reinforce correct use of those skills.

Processing: Processing will take place at the end of the activity with each group recording two things their group did very well and one thing they could work on for next time they meet. Also, the teacher will share feedback.

FUNCTION AND LOCATION OF BODY ORGANS
by
Lori Michelson

Subject Area: Science - Grade 6

Assigned Roles: Researcher/Runner, Recorder, Reader

Background: Elementary age students are being presented information dealing with the human body in relation to drug and alcohol abuse, often with little knowledge of how a healthy body should function. By learning the operations of basic organs, students will better understand the importance of taking care of themselves.

I. Decisions

Lesson: The learner will recognize the body organ, function of, and location of.

Group Size: 3-4

Group Assignment:
Use books to name body organ - Label - Write function of. Cut out - Place on full size body in proper place.

Materials: Health books, body books, set of papers, one large sheet of paper.

II. Set the Lesson

Academic Task:
Make a body containing heart, lungs, stomach, intestines, and liver. Write the function on the organ and place properly on full-size traced body.

Criteria for Success:
All organs labeled correctly and placed on body in proper areas. 4/5 - 90% (A), 3/5 - 85% (B).

Positive Interdependence:
All must know name and function of organ.

Individual Accountability:
Anyone I call on will be able to tell me the organ and function of it.

Expected Behaviors:
Work in your group.
Share your knowledge in your group.
Encourage each other.

III. Monitoring

Will be done by teacher.

Focus will be on individuals.

Observation sheet includes the behaviors of: Staying in group. Sharing and encouraging.

Processing/Feedback: Review each group's completed project. Are all parts correctly named, functions, and in proper body area?

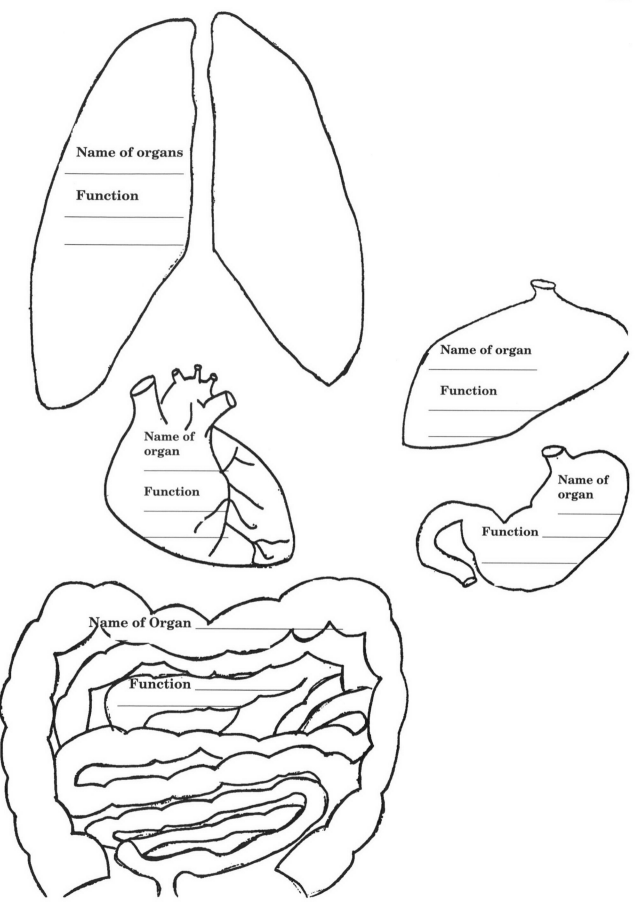

Name of organs

_____

Function

_____

_____

Name of organ

_____

Function

_____

_____

Name of
organ

_____

Function

_____

_____

Name of
organ

Function _____

_____

Name of Organ _____

Function _____

_____

HOW DOES COLOR HELP AN ANIMAL TO SURVIVE?
by
Maureen Macdonald

I. Decisions

Group Assignments: Counting Off

Materials: 30 red, 30 green, 30 blue, 30 yellow toothpicks, 1 square meter of green cloth, timer, and worksheet.

Group Roles: Investigator: prepares the materials. Manger: collects as many "insects" as possible in 15 seconds. Recorder: records the numbers of the different colored toothpicks collected and writes answers to the questions on worksheet.

II. Academic Task

Students are to pretend that the cloth is grass, the toothpicks are insects, and the Manager is a bird looking for insects. After the cloth is spread out and the toothpicks scattered, the manager will have 15 seconds to pick up as many "insects" as possible, one at a time. Allow each student to have a turn as the Manager— the teacher will assign the new roles.

III. Criteria for Success

Students will be able to explain how color can help an animal survive and give examples of other animals that use color to survive.

IV. Positive Interdependence
   A. I will collect one sheet from the group with the group member' names.
   B. Each student will have a role within the group.
   C. Each group will be able to tell of three other examples of animals that use color as a means to survive.

V. Individual Accountability
   A. The teacher will call on any member of the group to give an example of animals that use color to survive.
   B. The teacher will also call on any member of the group to answer the questions on the worksheet.
   C. Students will be tested on this concept on a test at the end of the chapter.

VI. Expected Behaviors
   A. Students will take turns within their groups.
   B. Students will use 6" voices.
   C. Students will thank one another at the end of the lesson.

VII. Monitoring

The teacher will walk around the room to monitor students within their groups.

The teacher will reward those groups using the expected behaviors with a sticker.

VIII. Processing

The teacher will process at the end of the lesson by praising those groups that demonstrated the expected behaviors.

Groups will also process by explaining what they felt they did well and something they feel they can work on in future groups.

LABORATORY SAFETY
by
Lisa Dumphey

Grade Level: 8th

Subject Area: Physical Science

Step 1.   Select a lesson: Laboratory Safety

Step 2.   Make Decisions
   a. Group Size: 3-4
   b. Assignment to Groups: Random selection by numbered index cards.
   c. Room Arrangement: Lab tables will be left as is and students will move chairs.
   d. Materials needed for each group: book, paper, and pencil for each person.
   e. Assigning Roles: No roles will be used for this lesson.

Step 3.   Set the Lesson.

   a. Task: Today we will be learning about laboratory safety. The first rule of laboratory safety is know what you are doing. This textbook uses several safety symbols to alert you to possible laboratory dangers. You need to understand each symbol before you can begin any investigation.

   In our lesson today you will be learning safety symbols and their meaning. Your job as a group is to make sure that all the members understand the symbols. Think of things that will help you remember. At the end of the period you will be having a quiz over the symbols and their meaning. Those groups in which all of the members receive a 100% on their quiz will receive bonus points. If you finish early, try to think of other areas in which symbols are used for safety reasons. I also want to remind you that I will be listening for 12" voices.

   b. Positive interdependence:
   Students are working towards a common learning goal and reward.

   c. Individual accountability:
   Students will be receiving a quiz over the material at the end of period.

   d. Criteria for success:
   The grades students receive on the test and the behaviors shown during group work will determine their success.

   e. Specific behaviors expected:
    Since this will be done at the beginning of the year I will be looking for quiet voices and whether students can go quietly to their groups.

Step 4.   Monitor and Process

   a. Evidence of expected behaviors: I should notice students using 12" voices. I should also notice students moving quickly and quietly to their groups.

   b. Observation form: Walking from group to group and giving extra point cards if they are working with 12" voices.

   c. Plans for processing: We will have a discussion on their behavior when the group work is completed. I will ask them to rank their group on how well they thought they did on 12" voices.

Step 5.   Evaluate Outcomes

   Will be done after lesson is actually given.

PROTECTION OF OUR ENVIRONMENT - RECYCLING
by
Jeff Amey

Grade: 7 - 12

Content: Science

Group Size: Teams of four

Assigned Roles: Research director, recorder, presenter, and organizer of facts.

Background: (Universal for all grades) Students are challenged to develop and create products utilized by consumers that are constructed of recycled material. Students are called on to "stretch imaginations" as they visualize what could be used to form and strengthen various products from recyclable material.

Materials: Pencils and paper, research books, environmental science books, earth science and chemistry books, poster paper and graph paper.

Set: Begin by making available to students lists of material that are environmentally "safe" and products that are of a recyclable material. Using these lists, develop new products, showing how they are made and the energy saved via the process used to make that new product.

Objective: To develop in the minds of students that the environment is a delicate instrument and the quality of life depends upon what science and technology explore that will determine the quality of life for future generations. Understanding conversion of fuel to energy and the expending of that resource and how it relates to the environment.

Task: The problem with "What do you do with un-recyclable material?" confronts mankind. Set up a model of existence in a small community in which all consumer products could be broken down and reused and nothing would be forced from the earth again. Each team member will contribute to the project. Teams will present project on third day. Charts and graphs will be needed to develop visuals to communicate any ideas. Pictures or artwork demonstrating product and product line will further the process of visual presentation.

Processing: Groups work together during the last 20 minutes to pull information together. Suggestions on redirection would apply at this time.

Assignment: This assignment will be presented after the third day. Closure is necessary on each working session.

Closure: After presentations, each group as an audience will be allowed to bring out the strong points of the other's presentation.

Students may also express similarities and differences in each other's findings.

SCIENCE CHAPTER REVIEW
by
Angela Jacobs

Grade Level: Intermediate

Subject Area: Science

Step 1. Select a Lesson

Students work cooperatively on completing three parts of a chapter review.

Step 2. Make Decisions
a. Group size: Three
b. Assignment to groups: Teacher assigned, according to ability. One high student, one medium and one low.
c. Room arrangement: Desks arranged in threes. Entire room is arranged in a horseshoe configuration.
d. Materials needed for each group: Science text, notebooks, and a pen.
e. Assigning roles: Reporter: Explains his/her section. Encourager: Asks questions, praises reporters' information. Observer: Completes part of observation sheet, looking for use of praise questions and quality of information. Roles change every 15 minutes.

Step 3. Set the Lesson. State, in language your students understand.
a. Task: Students are to relay each section of prepared review information to group members. Group will apply information to test material.
b. Positive interdependence: Each member should gain an understanding of all three sections of the chapter and apply it to similar test questions.
c. Individual accountability: Each student will be tested individually on the information in the chapter.
d. Criteria for success: All group members should score an 80% or higher on the test. This would demonstrate a good understanding of all three sections of information.
e. Specific behaviors expected: Each member should share quality information with the group. Members should ask questions and praise the reporter.

Step 4. Monitor and Process
a. Evidence of expected behaviors (appropriate actions): Each group has an index card with members' names on it. Stickers will be placed on cards when appropriate behaviors are observed.
b. Observation form: Checks for: praising, questioning, and retaining quality information.
c. Plans for processing (feedback): Groups share their recordings, teacher inputs her ideas (from observation sheet).

Step 5. Evaluate Outcomes
a. Task achievement: Within the group, review observation checklist and teacher response.
b. Group functioning: Group can summarize their reactions to what took place during review including ideas for improvement.
c. Notes on individuals: Can be kept on a checklist with marks for appropriate behaviors during group work.
d. Suggestions for next time: concentrate on appropriate behaviors. Learn through group interaction and class responses to activities.

THE EARTH'S BIOMES
by
Donna Gachev

Grade: Self-contained sixth

Subject Area: Science

Step 1: Lesson Selection

These are lessons that will be based on an entire unit in Science. The unit is called THE EARTH'S BIOMES (HABITATS). This is one activity that may last up to several days. (Jigsaw lesson)

Step 2: Decision Making
    a. Group Size: The groups will be divided into four groups of six or the number of biomes you would like presented within that unit.
    b. Group Assignments: The students will initially be assigned to their groups by using the following randomly selected technique: This group is called their "BASE GROUP."

Choose six parts of speech, for example, NOUNS, VERBS, ADJECTIVES, ADVERBS, PRO-NOUNS, and PREPOSITIONS. For each category, write out on cards a word having that part of speech. Shuffle the 24 cards and pass them out to the students. The teacher will then direct all NOUNS, for example, to go to a certain set of desks which will result in a randomly selected group.

As the lesson progresses other groups need to be constituted randomly.

    c. Room Arrangement: Prior to selecting the actual groups, students are asked to move their desks in six groups of four.

    d. Materials: 24 science books, 24 pencils, 24 notebooks, 4 sets consisting of 6 biome pictures (one set per group), construction paper, 6 black markers (one per group) and 6 bottles of glue (one per group)

    e. Assigning Roles: The following four roles will be assigned (one per student) only when the base groups come together to work on their final project (last lesson).

> 1. TRAVELER - A designated person in a group that is allowed to ask the teacher questions and/or obtain materials (glue, for example) for their group.

> 2. TIME KEEPER/MANAGER - A designated student that keeps time and pace for their group.

> 3. PRINTER/WRITER - A person chosen to take charge of putting the group's notes into print after a group consensus has been reached.

> 4. PASTE ARTIST - This person is given the job of ensuring that a consensus is achieved before placing and gluing picture(s).

Step 3: State the Lesson

a. Task: There are 6 tasks involved in this activity.

1. Each individual within a group is assigned to read one of the six Biomes presented in unit three of their science books. The teacher will randomly count off all the members in the groups and then give each number the pages that are to be read. For example, all number ones read pages 132-135 on the Tundra Biome.

2. Each child is to take notes on what he or she reads. The notes will include three main topics: 1) Defining all bold-face words, 2) Recording two fun facts about their biome, and 3) Listing seven most important characteristics that identifies their biome and (optional) any other pertinent information.

3. A group having similar numbers/biomes come together after independent reading and note taking have been completed. The six groups of four now formed are to share and edit their notes and come to a consensus about what to write as final notes for their designated section. It is expected that the children will alter their notes accordingly so that when they return to their "base" groups, the same information about each biome is taught.

4. The six groups of four that are formulated in the above task are now divided into 12 groups of two. A pair is made up by having each child look for a partner that has the nearest birth date to his or her own.

The task designed for the partners is to review the material and figure out a good way to go back to their "base" group in order to teach them their particular biome.

5. In their original "base" groups, each child takes a turn teaching their group about their biome. Additional notetaking is optional for each student.

6. As they remain in their original "base" group of four, the teacher asks each group to complete the following project: it is at this time the roles are given to each of the children. Selecting the children for the roles will again be done randomly. For example, the youngest is the time keeper. The person to the left is the ....etc.

The project consists of making a BIOME BOOK that consists of all notes taken by each biome representative and the pictures given to each group illustrating all the biomes. The teacher will model a Biome Identification Book and discuss possible procedures for making it. Variations on the final product will also be discussed with the entire class. The teacher may also include an assignment sheet that lists the contents that need to be constructed in each group's Biome Book. For example, title of biome, picture(s) of the biome, seven identifiable traits of the biome, etc....

b. Positive Interdependence: The following reflects the interdependence that exists? 1) Each student is responsible for learning the entire unit. Each student will learn by depending on classmates to give him/her the accurate information needed to pass the test, 2) Each student is also responsible for making sure that his fellow peers learn the material he or she has presented, and 3) Each person has a role to play that is crucial in completing one single product per group.

c. Individual Accountability: Not only are they individually accountable for the roles they play in their groups, but most importantly they're solely accountable for the Science post-test.

d. Criteria for Success: The teacher will clearly explain the criteria in the beginning of the first lesson.

1. As a whole class their criterion will be that the mean class score averages out to be better than their last science test mean. If this is met, each student will get bonus points to be added onto that test.

2. Their group criterion also pertains to collecting additional points to that test paper. It happens when all the members in a group obtain a mean average score of at least 85%.

3. Finally, each person alone can raise their test paper even higher if they had done better than their last science test.

e. Expected Behaviors: The two general cooperative skills expected in this activity, as well as specified in detail on a T CHART and discussed early on, are as follows:

1. Check to make sure everyone in the group understands the material and agrees with the way it is being presented.

2. Encourage peers to participate.

Step 4: Monitor and Process

a. Evidence of Expected Behaviors: Not only will the expected behaviors be listed on the board, but included with that will be T- CHARTS. The charts will be constructed by a short brainstorming activity the entire class will do by elaborating more specifically on the expected behaviors the teacher first defines.

b. Observation Form and Observer(s): Both the teacher and class will be held accountable for observing the appropriate behaviors displayed in group.

As for the teacher, a form is made up consisting of all the student names and all the cooperative skills that are taught in that semester. The teacher will indicate to the class that only four students will be observed during group work for the cooperative skills discussed in class. All students should remain alert because they do not know which four children are chosen until the end of each lesson.

c. Processing Plans (Feedback): For the teacher, the above form would be used as a guideline to indicate which children are in need of additional guidance. Checking off and tallying what behaviors were demonstrated is one way to use the form.

In addition to using the observation sheet, the students will be asked to assess their entire group's behavior using the T CHARTS. The group will be asked to come to a consensus about how well they have done. After a few minutes of general discussion, the teacher will identify one child to be the speaker for their group.

Step 5: Evaluate Outcomes

A. TASK ACHIEVEMENT

B. GROUP FUNCTIONING

C. INDIVIDUAL NOTES

D. SUGGESTIONS FOR NEXT TIME

To be evaluated after all lessons of the activity have been completed.

VERTEBRATES IN SCIENCE
by
Margaret Mohr

Grade Level: 5th

Subject Area: Science (vertebrates)

I. **Lesson:** Characteristics of the five vertebrate groups: fish, amphibians, reptiles, birds, mammals. (Jigsaw lesson)

II. a. **Group size:** 5 in base, 6 in second group
    b. **Assignment to groups:** random
    c. **Room arrangement:** desk groups of 5
    d. **Materials needed for each group:** Two pieces of paper and pen/pencil per student, text book, reference material.
    e. **Assigning roles:** Each member has the same role which is to learn information away from the base group and teach base group members using a jigsaw strategy.

III. a. **Task:** Each student in the base group of 5 will choose one of the five vertebrate groups to become an <u>expert</u> on. They will be assigned the following numbers to correspond with each animal group 1 - fish, 2 - amphibians, 3 - reptiles, 4 - birds, 5 - mammals. Each student will leave the base group to meet with the rest of the students having the same number/animal group. In this larger group, all the "fish," for example, will use reference books and the science text to list physical characteristics of the "fish" group. After they have all become <u>experts</u> on fish through peer questioning and coaching, they will return to base groups and teach these characteristics to fellow base group members who will take notes.
     b. **Positive Interdependence:** Each member will turn in notes on all five animal groups, each member should be able to list characteristics of any of the five groups when asked at random.
     c. **Individual Accountability:** Each member is expected to learn information and teach this to others. This information will be on a quiz the following day.
     d. **Criteria for Success:** If all group members receive a 90% or better on the quiz, bonus points will be awarded. As a whole group, make a master chart for each vertebrate group listing characteristics.
     e. **Specific behaviors expected:** 12 inch voices, listen carefully and respectfully, contribute ideas.

IV. a. **Evidence of Expected Behaviors:** Appropriate use of voice; see that one person is talking at a time and others are listening intently.
    b. **Observation form:** Teacher observation
    c. **Plans for processing:** Write expected behaviors on board before group work begins and refer back to them at end of activity, discuss as large group choosing random individuals to report.

V. **Task Achievement:** As a whole class, develop a master chart for each vertebrate group listing characteristics.

Social Studies

**With heads together and 12" voices
a triad becomes an intense huddle.**

CURRENT EVENTS

by
Beth Boos

Grade: 6 - 9

Content: Social Studies

Group Size: Teams of five

Background:

It is important that middle school students become and remain aware of the events that are happening around them at the local, state, and national levels and around the world. By being knowledgeable about current events and encouraging the students to continue their interest, their citizenship skills will benefit.

Materials: One newspaper.

Set: Select five articles to be investigated by students. Divide class in groups of five. Have students number themselves 1-5. Then, "jigsaw" into five groups for their "research" groups. Then, students will return back to their original group (sharing group).

Objective: At the end of this activity students will become familiar with the day's current events as each child will participate in sharing their information and reactions regarding each article.

Task:

Jigsaw Strategy

After the students are assembled in their groups, each group will be assigned one article to read looking for main ideas. During a period of approximately ten minutes, each student will become an "expert" regarding their article. Each student should record important information to take back to the home base groups. At the end of the ten minute segment, students will re-group with a representative from each of the previous groups to share their knowledge as an "expert."

Processing: To process effectively, ask students to turn to others in their group and discuss:

1. Why they were good at their jobs.
2. How it felt to teach others.

Assignment: This lesson will take one class period with part of the time spent in their "research" group and the other time spent in their "sharing" group.

Closure: After spending time in both the "research" and the "sharing" groups, the instructor will spend the remainder of the class period reviewing each of the articles and hearing any final discussions regarding each one.

DISCUSSING WORLD PROBLEMS

by
Michelle Pierre

I. Decisions:

Lesson: Social Studies - After the class has discussed Phoenix (or any other major city) and its growth problems, the students will discuss world problems and form some solutions.

Group Size: Students will be in groups of four.

Group Assignments:
Teacher selects groups (1 high, 2 average, and 1 low achieving student per group). Roles: Materials Handler, Encourager, Writer/Recorder.

Materials: Each group has the problem/solution worksheet.

II. Set the Lesson:

Academic Task:
The students will complete a worksheet comprised of a list of world problems.

1. Rank order 10 world problems from most important to least important.
2. Select one problem and brainstorm for solutions.

Criteria for Success:
The groups will come to a consensus ranking the problems. At least 10 items will be listed as solutions. 10 items - 100%, 9 - 90%, 8 - 80%, 7 - 70%, 6 - 60%, 5 or below - F.

Positive Interdependence:
The group will share one paper for one grade.

Individual Accountability:
Each student must contribute at least two items for the list. Give two tokens to each student to track the number of contributions made. Material Handler is responsible for tokens. Later I will call on people at random to discuss solutions.

Expected Behaviors:

1. Students will discuss the problems and share at least 2 items for the list.

2. Students will ask questions to find out what classmates think or to have them further explain their views.

3. Students will encourage others to share and praise each other for good ideas.

III. Monitoring:

Monitoring will be done by the teacher.

Focus will be on individuals and individual groups.

Observation sheet includes the behaviors of: 1) Shares ideas, 2) Asks questions, and 3) Encourages/praises others.

Processing/Feedback: The teacher will have each group meet to go over their evaluation sheets. The group's cooperation and expected behaviors will be discussed.

MAP AND MEMORY SKILLS

by
Daniel J. Malmberg

Grade Level: 6-8

Subject Area: Geography

Lesson Summary: Group members work cooperatively to learn the names and locations of the countries in Central America and any other continent/region, and ensure that all group members can successfully complete an outline map of the region. Also, students will use memorization strategies suggested by the teacher or develop new strategies.

Instructional Objectives: The purpose of this lesson is to introduce the students to the Central American region, to give students the practice necessary to become familiar with the names and locations of the countries in that region, and to allow students to experiment with new memorization strategies.

Time Required: 30-40 minutes

Materials: Grouping cards, one outline map per group, and one text per group.

Group Assignments: Students will be assigned to groups randomly by drawing a card from the teacher. There will be three types of cards: a map card, a flag card, and a capital city card. All students with cards from the same country will become a group.

Roles: Recorder: Records the information on the map and the techniques employed in the group's memorization strategy. Researcher/Encourager: Looks up the information from the text and also encourages members to share their ideas. Checker: Checks to make sure the information is properly placed on the map, and that all members understand and can explain the strategy used by the group for mastery of the information.

> The student with:
> Map Card = Recorder
> Flag Card = Researcher/Encourager
> Capital Card = Checker

Instructional Task:

1. Fill in the outline map using the book for references.

2. Use or develop a strategy to memorize the names and locations of the seven countries in Central America.

3. Each member must be able to:

   —explain the strategy used by the group.

   —help produce a class map on the overhead projector.

   —fill in an outline map for a quiz.

Positive Interdependence:

1. The students will work face to face with one map and one text.

2. The students will share their ideas on strategies for learning the material.

3. Each member should be able to explain the strategy used by the group.

4. Each member should be able to fill in the outline map.

5. Bonus points will be awarded to students in groups where each member successfully completes the map.

Individual Accountability: At the end of the lesson, each student must be able to explain the method used by his/her group for mastering the material. Each student must also be prepared to come to an overhead map and name and locate one of the countries. Every student should be able to fill in the outline map the following day for the quiz.

Criteria for Success: Success will be determined by each group member's ability to complete the outline map quiz. 100% Fantastic + Bonus Points.

Expected Behaviors: A T-Chart will be used to inform students of the expected behaviors.

Expect to see:

— students sitting face to face.

— all members participating - leaning in and making eye contact.

— each member fulfilling his/her role.

Expect to hear:

— quiet voices.

— compliments for good ideas.

— a "thank you" for group members' help.

Monitoring and Processing: Monitoring will be done by the teacher signing an observation sheet for each group. The teacher will watch to see how the students work together and take time to praise appropriate behaviors. Processing will be done at the end of the lesson with students rating their performance as a group. The groups should consult the T-Chart before evaluating. Groups will be asked to choose a skill to work on for the next class.

NATURAL RESOURCES
by
Carrie Van Zeeland

Grade Level: 6-8

Subject Area: Social Studies

Lesson Objectives: All students will demonstrate knowledge of how our most important natural resources are being abused and what part they can play in the correction and prevention of this abuse.

Time Required: Up to three 30-minute sessions.

Group Size: Groups of three, if possible.

Assignment to Group: Distribute an index card to each student. Each card has the name of a storybook character on it. Ask students to find and form a group with the characters from the same story. Once their group is established, they find a spot on the floor and sit face-to-face.

Roles: Their roles are determined by the letter found in the upper right hand corner of their index card, either A, B, or C.

    A. Recorder—Lists all the ways, suggested by the group, in which their natural resource is being abused or how it could be conserved.
    B. Writer—Writes down the groups' ideas for characters and the lines they will say in the skit they will develop.
    C. Director—Makes final decisions and settles any disputes.

Materials: The Recorder and Writer need a pencil and paper. The Director chooses from a group of index cards which natural resource they have and whether their skit has to show a) how the natural resource is being abused or b) what is or should be done to conserve this natural resource.

Task: Each group is responsible for acting out a 2-3 minute skit which demonstrates their knowledge of either how the natural resource they chose is being abused or how it can be conserved.

Positive Interdependence: The list of brainstormed ideas and the script is to be turned before the skit is performed. The skit's success is judged by:

    A.   Participation of all group members.
    B.   Proof of comprehension of previously learned material through lessons and
        research papers on selected natural resources.

Each member will be assigned a role, as outlined earlier. Each role must be performed the set order, and must be a collaboration of all group members' efforts. If a group has only two members, the student who is the Recorder is also the Director.

Individual Accountability: Randomly choosing students to answer questions reviewing material learned through each others' skits.

Each student takes a comprehensive test individually.

Criteria for Success: Test Scores   93% - Excellent
                                            87% - Very Good
                                            83% - Satisfactory

Expected Behaviors:

    A.   All members are distributing ideas for the Recorder and Writer to use in their rough drafts of the group's plan.

    B.   Members are working quietly.

Evidence: I will be looking and listening for the following: members leaning in, sharing of ideas, suggestions made positively, only constructive criticism, and quiet voices.

Intervening: I will be circulating and monitoring accomplishments of each group, noting steady progress from listing ideas to writing of the script, to practicing the skit.

Processing: Collect papers at end of each 30-minute period. Randomly and without singling out any individual, comment on progress that was made and behaviors that were observed. Discuss what was done well and what needs to be improved during next session.

PLAYING GAMES WITH MOTHER EARTH
by
Bill Ball

Grade: 7 - 9

Content: Social Studies

Group Size: Four to five

Assigned Roles:
>   Recorder, Reporter

Background:

>   Students comprise an active group of individuals. Their activities take them into many parts of the environment for their work and recreation.

>   By building activities within the group, the members will be able to tell the difference between games and work activities that damage the environment.

Materials: Pencils, paper, newspaper photographs and access to going outside.

Set: To set the stage, the teacher will divide the class into teams of four to five students. Half of each team will do one of the following: By hypothesizing and brainstorming, draw a picture on a poster depicting the theme: <u>Play Lightly on the Earth</u>. The second half of the same team will follow the same procedure, but they will base their picture theme on <u>Play Hard on the Earth</u> (Play will be defined as recreation).

>   The recorder of each half will write a short summary of the team's picture.

Objective: The student teams will be able to:

>   a. Tell the difference between games that are harmful and
>   not harmful to the environment.

>   b. Invent games with a non-negative effect on the environment.

Task: Students will look for evidence of games that are harmful to the environment. The student teams will invent and play games that have a benign effect on the environment.

Processing:

>   a.   Go outside anywhere in the community and look for evidence of games that have caused damage to the environment. Students should write down possible reasons for these damages, and how they could have been prevented.

>   b.   Teacher introduces the concept of games that do no harm to the environment.

>   c.   Ask the students to work together in their teams, to invent a game that does no serious harm to the environment.

>   d.   Each team presents a game to the others and plays it.

Closure: Ask students to discuss their reactions to the games and to talk about their feelings concerning the importance of playing games that do little or no damage to the environment.

PROBLEM SOLVING "WHAT IF....?"
by
Mary Smith

Grade: 6-7

Content: Social Studies/History

Group size: Teams of Three

Assigned roles:

        Scribe: Records Information
        Orator: Public Speaker
        Historian: Gathers Resources

Background:

        Middle grade students tackle an endless stream of challenges as they problem-solve through the social maze seeking peer approval. By structuring constructive controversies within subject matter, teens learn to turn peer pressure into peer power as they navigate the steps of problem solving.

Materials: Pencil and paper

Set: To set the stage for this problem solving lesson, ask students to relate a personal vignette that illustrates this quote:

        Trust is the result of a risk successfully survived!—Jack R. Gibb

        After sufficient partner interaction, sample volunteers for their personal vignettes.

Objective: The students will practice the explicit thinking skills (i.e. brainstorming, hypothesizing, and predicting outcomes) and their implicit thinking skills (i.e. consensus seeking, projecting and summarizing) by writing an essay using the "What if" activity.

Task: Explain to the students that they are to problem-solve some of history's most notorious "What ifs." For example, what if......

        ..... the South had won?

        ..... the Indians had kept their land?

        ..... women still could not vote?

        ..... there had been no Berlin Wall?

        ..... the Roman Empire had not fallen?

        Assign teams of three the roles needed:

        Scribe: Records information

        Orator: Public speaker

        Historian: Gathers information

The first problem-solving task is to "brainstorm" a list of "What ifs" from history while the historian in the group scans the history book and reviews old notes.

Once a list is made in each group, have each team evaluate its ideas and select a favorite "what if" to work with. Each group is expected to have criteria for its final selection and be ready to justify its choice.

Have students web possible outcomes to their "What ifs" from history. Using responses in turn, each group should jot down seven to ten ideas.

Using their selected "what if" scenarios, all students should write a brief essay. First, they should write from the eyes of a participant. That is, as a journal entry, rewrite the endings of the "What ifs" as they might have been. They should personify with actions and feelings, the words one may have written to describe the hypothesized outcomes of the "what ifs". Second, students should project the scenario into the present to describe how things would be if the "what if" had occurred.

After students have had sufficient opportunity to complete their individual assignments, have team members select an appropriate journal selection from their group that will give the audience the "revised" picture of history as presented in the "what if" assignment.

Next, have the orators read the "capsules" of the personal journal entries to give the audience a flavor of how things would be different.

Processing: To process effectively, ask students to turn to their groups and discuss:

1) how it feels to "walk in another's shoes," and

2) some of the emotions felt as they tried to think and behave as the other person.

Assignment:

This lesson may spill over into two days (or even more) depending on the purpose. If it does, remember to process and use closure at the end of each working session. Sample Processing Statement—We really needed someone to ....

Closure: As a class, discuss the "what ifs" selected and try to decide which "what if" would have caused the most dramatic difference today.

Next, have them discuss some "what ifs" thinking in other contexts such as:

Life: What if you want to change your hair style?

Math: What if we all used the metric system?

Science: What if the ozone layer does disappear?

Finally, have the students rate the "what if" activity as a problem solving strategy.

REVIEW UNIT ON ROMAN EMPIRE
by
Jean Robinson

I. Decisions:

Lesson: Review unit on Roman Empire - 1) Review important facts about life during
Roman Empire - prepare as a group for quiz. 2) Group project—plan oral presentation on family, social, and government life of Roman people.

Group Size: Groups of four

Group Assignments:
Teacher assigned student groups.

Materials: Text, packet of information on Roman Empire, Book of Roman plays, use of
Media Center for research.

II. Set the Lesson:

Academic Task:
1. Plan group oral presentation on some aspect of life during Roman Empire.
2. Review important facts about Roman Empire for quiz.

Criteria for Success:
Student will be aware of success by oral presentation or speech on Roman Empire.
Student will know grade on Review Quiz.

Positive Interdependence:
The group will plan presentation as a team. They will plan and prepare for quiz as a
team. 10 extra points if team as a whole does C or above on quiz.

Individual Accountability:
Individual part of speech and individual score on quiz.

Expected Behaviors:

1. Working as a group using quiet voices.
2. Social skills—getting along, encouraging, helping each other.
3. Asking each other questions or quizzing each other.

III. Monitoring:

Monitoring will be done by:
Teacher/Student

Focus will be on:
Individuals and individual groups.

Observation sheet includes the behaviors of:
See expected social behaviors (above).

Processing/Feedback:
Take time to meet with each group - going over observation sheet - and allow for students
to plan how to make improvements both personal and as a group.

SOCIAL STUDIES UNIT - GREECE
by
Donna H. Turner

Objective: To develop an understanding of the concept of democracy.

To learn about and to contrast and compare the governmental structures of Athens and Sparta.

To understand how the government in Greece, so long ago, is responsible for our system of democracy today.

Vocabulary: Group #1 Constitution
Democracy
Representative democracy (context)

Group #2 Ostracized
Assembly
Population

Group #3 Ephors (ee fors)
Senate - (What did it do?--1.2.,)

Group #4 Council
Rule of Kings

Group #5 Democracy (What are the two root Greek words? What do they mean?)

Group #6 Tyrants
Council of 500

Group #7 Ostracon (Explain what this is.)
Ostracized

Group #8 Proud
Modern democracy

1. Review how our government in the United States is set up. On board, put the heading OUR GOVERNMENT.

2. Ask: What is the document under which we are governed? (Constitution) Put on board. (Constitution).

What does the Constitution contain? (Rules and a system of basic principles that we live by.) Put on board.

Who is responsible for carrying out the laws? (President and the Legislative branch of our government.)

What makes up the Legislative Branch of our government? (Senate and House of Representatives.) Put on board.

1. Senate:

> Elected directly
> Must be 30 to serve
> Whole state has only two

2. House of Representatives

> We elect directly from   districts
> Must be 25 to serve

WHO CAN VOTE IN OUR SYSTEM: All men and women over 18 who have registered can vote.

Today we will look at how the ancient Greeks governed themselves, specifically Athens and Sparta.

When we are finished our group work today, or tomorrow, we should be able to put on the board, how Athens and Sparta were governed, and how each compares to our system of government.

There will be three people in each group. #1 will be the reader; you will read the paragraphs assigned to you out loud as the other two members follow along. #2 will be the recorder—responsible for putting the important ideas down on paper. (You will have a sheet to help you do this.) #3 will be our word expert who will look up any words the group does not understand plus the words assigned to your group.

Groups: #s 1,2,3 will all contribute ideas from the reading to answer the directed reading activity your group will receive. One copy per group. When the directed reading activity is complete, you will all sign the top. When you sign the top it means you agree that the answers on the sheet are correct.

Important information that each group should have is outlined on the following pages. The form of a Direct Reading Activity helps focus in on what the students need to know.

Directed Reading Activity

Vocabulary: 1. Constitution

2. Democracy

3. Representative Democracy

1. How was Athens governed?

2. What was the government of Athens based on?

3. The government provided for an _____.

4. The _____ was made up of all the citizens of Athens. (_____ only)

5. The Athenian constitution provided for a _____ of 500 chosen by the _____ tribes of Athens.

6. The council was very _____.

7. It decided: 1.

2.

8. Why did they keep watch over the officials?

9. In choosing leaders to represent themselves, the Council of 500 was a good example of a _____.

Directed Reading Activity

Vocabulary: 1. Ostracized

2. Assembly

3. Population

1. The everyday business of governing Athens was done by _____ _____.

2. The leader of the generals was often the real _____ of Athens.

3. The leaders could not become too powerful or evil. Any leader could be _____ by being ordered to leave Athens.

4. Sparta was NOT ruled by a _____, although it did have a _____.

5. The Spartan constitution provided for an _____. All _____ _____ at least _____ years old belonged to it.

6. That meant that only _____ Spartan men belonged to the Assembly.

Directed Reading Activity

Vocabulary: Ephors

Senate—What did it do?

1.

2.

1. The _____elected _____men called _____ each year, and they ran the government.

2. In addition the Spartans had two _____, the title of which was handed down to sons.

3. In times of war, the kings acted as _____.

4. The kings had little real _____.

5. Sparta also had a _____.

6. This _____ was made up of _____men who were at least _____ years old.

7. The Senate acted as a _____ for _____ _____.

8. The Senate also suggested what _____the Assembly out to _____.

Directed Reading Activity

Vocabulary: Council

Rule of Kings

1. Sparta was really run by a _____ _____ of people.

2. It was run like an _____ _____ and had no real _____.

3. Athenians had more _____ and more _____ and Athens was more _____ than Sparta.

4. But Athens still had _____ on its democracy.

5. Athenian _____ and _____ had _____ on their rights. _____ had _____rights at all.

Directed Reading Activity

Vocabulary: Democracy is made op of two Greek
words. What are they?
What do they mean?

1. The _____ of _____is the greatest contribution made to the world by the _____

_____.

2. Greece was not always a _____. At first almost all the city-states were ruled by

_____.

3. Then a _____ could do exactly as he _____.

4. Later _____were set up to help the _____ rule.

5. The councils were controlled by _____ and _____ _____.

6. At about _____ B.C., the Athenian council got rid of the rule of kings.

7. _____arose who promised everything to everybody in order to win votes.

Directed Reading Activity

Vocabulary: Council of 500
Tyrants

1. When the _____ did get power, they often _____ as they pleased. These
leaders were called _____, meaning who rules _____ _____

_____.

2. The _____ were _____with rule by _____, especially in _____.

3. By _____B.C., the _____ in many city-states were driven from _____.

4. This is when the new system of _____ called _____ arose.

5. Democracy comes from two Greek words _____ _____, which mean _____

_____ _____ _____.

Directed Reading Activity

Group #7

Vocabulary: Ostracon
Ostracized
Amateurs

1. All Athenian _____ were expected to _____ _____ in the government by attending _____ meetings.

2. The governing body of Athens was the _____ _____ _____.

3. Athenians tried hard to make sure no _____ could be _____ or get too much power.

4. If the assembly felt a leader had become dangerous, they could _____ him.

5. This meant that the official's name would be put on a piece of broken _____. That was put in a _____. When there were ostracons in the container, the leader was _____.

6. That meant he had to leave _____ for _____years.

Directed Reading Activity

Group #8

Vocabulary: Proud
Modern Democracy

1. Athens was _____ of its _____.

2. But not everything was _____.

3. The _____ did not have equal _____ as citizens.

4. It was certainly a _____ world

5. Athenians also kept _____. These _____ had _____ _____ at all.

6. The democracy of Athens showed the way for _____ _____.

Evaluation

Now, with teacher guidance, put Athens and Sparta beside the information related to our government in the U.S.

After the students have completed the group work, have them come together as a class and each group give a report on what they have found. As they give their reports, have the recorder write under Athens or Sparta the information from their learning that deals with government.

Completed comparison should look something like this:

Athens:

Democracy based on constitution.

Provided for an Assembly made of of (males only) citizens of Athens.

Constitution provided for a Council of 500 chosen by the 10 tribes of Athens (similar to Districts in our government)

Council of 500 decided what could be voted on.

Council of 500 watched what officials were doing.

Gave citizens more rights but with it came responsibilities.

Athens did, however, put limits on its democracy.

Sparta:

Had a constitution but was not a democracy.

Had an Assembly. You had to be 30 and own land to belong to it. They were 8,000 out of 376 thousand people.

Assembly elected 5 men, called ephors, each year and they ran the government.

They also had two kings; in times of war, kings acted as generals.

Had a Senate made up of 38 men who were at least 60.

Senate acted as a court for major crimes. It also suggested what laws ought to be passed.

Point out how our form of government today has followed the governments of Greece from 500 B.C.

THE IMPENDING CRISIS: U.S. 1850-1865

by
Dennis Harvey

Grade Level: 8

Subject Area: U.S. History

Step 1.   **Select a lesson**

Step 2.   **Make decisions**
    a. Group size: three
    b. Assignment to groups: Teacher decides based on abilities, personalities
    c. Room arrangement: Put desks in groups of three
    d. Materials needed for each group: Several sets of encyclopedias; textbooks
    e. Assigning roles: Reader, recorder, encourager/presenter

Step 3.   **Set the lesson.** State in language your students understand:
    a. Task: Create a timeline of ten important events and persons for the period 1850-1865 in U.S. History.
    b. Positive interdependence: Must work together to gather information from materials: textbook, encyclopedias
    c. Individual accountability: Each must be able to relate to other members of group all timeline entries from memory.
    d. Criteria for success: (see c also); comparison with other groups' timelines.
    e. Specific behaviors expected: Active research for information and active discussion of data to determine what will finally be put on timeline. Consensus necessary.

Step 4.   **Monitor and process**
    a. Evidence of expected behaviors (appropriate actions): Uninhibited communication, compromise through persuasion.
    b. Observation form: simply check for above informally, elaborate where necessary.

Step 5.   **Evaluate outcomes**
    a. Task achievement: (A) Once each group is finished, compare timelines and create one class timeline on board from groups' entries and consensus from all groups. Have students copy this in notes and make part of next quiz. (B) Group must be prepared to explain reasons for its choices.
    b. Suggestions for next time: Teacher summarizes findings and, if necessary, amends final class timeline if for some reason an outstanding event is overlooked!

U.S. TIMELINES

by
Deborah L. Wood

Grade: 6 - 7

Content: Social Studies

Group Size: Two (partners)

Assigned Roles:

Recorder: Records information; Material Manager: Gathers resources and materials.

Background:

Students often dislike Social Studies since they do not see the connection between the past and what is now presently happening in their world. Involving students in constructing a timeline of important historical events helps students visualize and acknowledge the people who have molded our present day world, and how they can contribute and make a difference individually to our world's future.

Materials: Magazines, styrofoam sheets, glue, scissors, pencils, colored pencils, and clasps.

Set: To set the stage for this activity, I propose the idea, "If President Lincoln hadn't taken a stand on slavery, how do you think that would have affected our history?" Class discussion. Students propose other events which greatly influenced the direction of history.

Objective: The students will practice their research skills by locating historical events which have taken place during their particular time period. Students will be involved in the decision-making process by learning to select events according to their thinking of its importance or impact on U.S. History. (Partners are selected by research skill knowledge in order to aid those who are struggling in this area. Tasks are assigned and specifics given on quality of work.)

Task: Partners are to select their important events for their 50 year time period through conducting extensive research. Then the partners are to illustrate each event in the best way possible (i.e. magazines, drawings). They then mount illustrations on segments of timeline which will be connected and displayed for class reference. (Jigsaw Activity)

Processing: The partners will share their particular favorite historical event or historical person from their time period and share reasons for the choice.

Assignment:

This activity may take three to four days to allow sufficient time for research to be completed. At the end of each class, allow time for processing focusing on social skills (i.e. working together - 6" voices). (stem statements)

Closure: Each pair will share their portion of the timeline with the class. They will explain their choices of events and people to represent their time period in an oral presentation. As each pair finishes their presentation; they connect their portion to the timeline to see the sequence of our nation's history.

WHAT EGYPT GAVE THE WORLD

by
Marjorie Lewis

Grade: Sixth

Subject Area: Social Studies

I.   Decisions:

Group Size: Three students per group, called a "triad"

Assignment to Groups:
1. Get together with your group. (already established by the teacher)
2. Assign numbers to each person in the group, from 1 to 3.
3. On pages of the text select three sections: Assign 1, 2, 3 to each section of text. Each person should read the section that correlates with their number.
4. Each person will take notes on the key ideas in their section.
5. After all students are done (about 10 minutes), the groups will get back together. Sit in a circle. At this time, each person will go over the important ideas in their section and teach them to the other members of their group.
6. As each person speaks, the other group members should be listening and taking a few notes of key ideas they want to remember. (The teacher will walk around and allow approximately five minutes per person.)
7. If your group seems to be done before other groups are finished, take time reviewing for the quiz.
8. Take the quiz at the end of the lesson.

Materials: Each student should have their own book, paper for note taking, and a writing implement.

II.   Set the Lesson:

Academic Task:

In this lesson, Egypt is the topic. Students will be quizzed on one gift that Egypt gave to the world in each of these areas: measurement, writing, and medicine. They should be able to remember one of Egypt's contributions for each.

This same idea could be applied to other countries or topics.

Criteria for Success:

Individually the students should be able to name one contribution for each area listed above. If the student is not able to score 100% accuracy, they will retake the test the following day. In order for the group to be successful, each one of the students in the group must reach 100% accuracy on the first quiz opportunity, given at the end of this lesson.

Positive Interdependence:

Reward: If all group members receive 100% accuracy on the first attempt at the quiz, each group member will receive a certificate. Positive Resource: Each person in the group is responsible for one part of the lesson and must teach it to the others after studying itthemselves. Environmental: Each group must sit in a circle when they are presenting the material they have studied to the others.

Individual Accountability:
> Each student will be responsible to do their portion of the lesson in order for the group to reach its goal. Each student will also receive an individual score on their own quiz. If they do not get 100% accuracy, they will take the quiz again (and again) until they achieve 100% accuracy.

Expected Behaviors:
> Students will sit close enough together to use quiet voices andnot disturb other groups. Students will listen to other group members as the material is presented by each one.

III. Monitoring:

Monitoring will be done by the teacher, walking around and encouraging 12-inch voices, (previously used as an expected behavior). The teacher will tell the kids to move on to the next person in approximately five-minute intervals.

Focus will be on the individual groups, and whether or not the students are listening to the other group members as they present their material.

Observation sheet includes the behaviors of knees touching and making eye contact with group members as they are listening to the others present material.

Processing/Feedback: When all the students have turned in the quiz,t he class as a whole will discuss the following:

1. What helped our groups to learn the material?

2. What behaviors got in the way of our learning the material?

3. What could we do differently next time?

3577